Camilla

Camilla

A Biography of
Camilla Eyring Kimball

Caroline Eyring Miner
Edward L. Kimball

Deseret Book Company
Salt Lake City, Utah
1980

To the memory of
Caroline Romney and
Edward Christian Eyring

© 1980 Deseret Book Company
All rights reserved
Printed in the United States of America
ISBN 0-87747-845-7
Library of Congress Catalog Card No. 80-69723

Preface

Camilla Eyring Kimball is a kindly, unassuming, intelligent, independent, sensitive, honest, hardworking, tolerant, generous, spiritual woman, worthy of her good husband.

If one characteristic had to be chosen to sum up her personality, it might be that she is intensely alive. She has said, "Some people feel that their responsibilities stifle them. I feel that fulfilling obligations is the best way to grow. Any woman should be alive to opportunities—alive to public interests, to her family, to growth from Church service. I have no patience with women who find life boring. Life is so interesting, it just worries me that I cannot get done all the things I want desperately to do."

She has been a pacesetter for all Eyring brothers and sisters and for her own children. As a refugee from Mexico, she secured an education with great determination and sacrifice. She believes that a good education is the way to rise in the world. All her life she has remained intellectually alive, curious, and studious.

"Of all the institutions I know, the family is the one that is eternal," Camilla has said, "and the home is its haven." She cooks marvelously, runs her home efficiently, and welcomes family and friends. She likewise loves the earth and works it hard to produce vegetables, fruits, and flowers in her small yard.

The central jewel in her husband's crown, she has supported and sustained him in all his illnesses and discouraging times and in his spiritual challenges, from young husband and father to prophet, seer, and revelator of The Church of Jesus Christ of Latter-day Saints. Her support has made possible his great contributions to others. But Camilla has also assumed her own leadership responsibilities in church and community, never submerged in her husband's personality. She has her own spiritual life and has come to her own understanding and application of the command to love both God and neighbor. She acts upon the motto "Never suppress a generous thought."

The chapters that follow are in great part based on Camilla's own autobiographical writings and journals, set down for her family without thought of publication.

Nelle Spillsbury Hatch, *Colonia Juarez,* provided the major source for the history of that village. Additional information on Camilla's married life can be found in *Spencer W. Kimball* (Bookcraft, 1977), the biography of her husband.

At the first suggestion that this book be written, Camilla expressed great reluctance to let go a last vestige of privacy. The notion that people might be interested in her life flattered but surprised her. She acquiesced only after she was persuaded that from her story other women might take some encouragement.

My Beloved

By President Spencer W. Kimball

In writing a few lines as a tribute to my beloved
wife, Camilla Eyring Kimball, I am a little at a loss—not
for things to say, but to know which things would be
appropriate. It seems almost sacrilege to attempt it, so
wide and deep and sacred are the memories of our
long life together—more than six decades, time
enough for many lights and shadows, disappointments and ecstasies.

We have traveled over the earth together. We have
ridden camels near Cairo, climbed high mountains in
South America, gone deep into the catacombs of
Rome, and dug into the seething lava of Mount Vesuvius. We have been together in the fjords of south New
Zealand and those far north in Norway. We have explored the rivers of Babylon and climbed the ziggurats
of Ur. We have traversed the delta of the Amazon,
rediscovered Machu Picchu, and watched killer lions
and giraffes and elephants roam free in Africa. We
have flown in mail planes in Norway, little transport
planes in Honduras, and the largest jets over the great
mountains, oceans, rivers, cities, and plains of the wide
world. We have climbed ancient towers and ruins in
Central America and have flown low over the Angkor
Wat of Cambodia.

We have celebrated Christmas with the people of
Saigon and Singapore. We have knelt together in the
Garden of Gethsemane and climbed the Mount of
Olives and the Mount of Transfiguration. We have
read the New Testament together in the tomb and

bathed our feet in the Sea of Galilee.

Camilla has been by my side in every experience. We have buried our parents and other loved ones, and have given up our own little children prematurely born. We have been in the depths and soared to the heights.

She has trembled and prayed through many hours of heart and throat and brain surgery for me, and through the hours of surgery on the legs of our youngest. She showed her character and strength through those agonizing days of wonder and fear at the hospitals and then those tiring, never-ending days and nights of uncomplaining care. For the little fellow she changed his day braces to night splints, and she rubbed and massaged his limbs and bathed and rubbed and bound them. For me she constantly helped and encouraged in every illness.

Year after year she has served and treated and blessed. Here is the true mother, the loyal wife, the perfect nurse!

We have wept together and we have laughed together. We have seen the sublime and have suffered the grotesque. Our life has been full of fun in spite of all the sad and serious things. We have danced; we have sung; we have entertained; we have loved and been loved. With a wife like Camilla Eyring, life becomes inclusive, full, and abundant.

After we returned at midnight from a dancing party at the Governor's Mansion in Salt Lake City some years ago, I said to her as I helped her from the car, "Darling, you were the most beautiful woman there. Not one could hold a candle to you." "Ah," she said, "I know that isn't true, dear, but I love to hear it from you."

1

I was born December 7, 1894, in Colonia Juarez, Chihuahua, Mexico, to Edward Christian Eyring and Caroline Cottam Romney. My paternal grandfather was from Germany, his wife from Basel, Switzerland. On my mother's side I inherited English blood. In each line were converts to The Church of Jesus Christ of Latter-day Saints who made the trek across the plains as pioneers to Utah in the mid-1800s. Both my grandfathers lived in St. George, Utah, both were polygamists, and both moved to Mexico to escape the danger of arrest for violation of the federal laws that had been passed making the practice of plural marriage a crime in the territories. For this reason I was born a Mexican citizen.

The Church, wishing to establish colonies where Saints could safely maintain their polygamous households, sent families into the Mexican state of Chihuahua, just south of New Mexico Territory. They ultimately established eight colonies—Juarez, Dublan, and Diaz east of the Sierra Madres; Chuichupa, Pacheco, and Garcia in the mountains; and Morelos and Oaxaca across the mountains in Sonora. Of these Juarez and Dublan were largest.

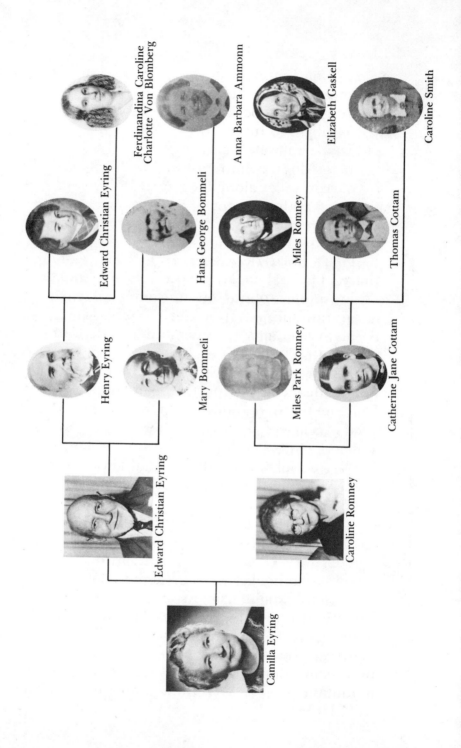

Ferdinandina Caroline
Charlotte Von Blomberg

Anna Barbara Ammonn

Elizabeth Gaskell

Caroline Smith

Edward Christian Eyring

Hans George Bommeli

Miles Romney

Thomas Cottam

Henry Eyring

Mary Bommeli

Miles Park Romney

Catherine Jane Cottam

Edward Christian Eyring

Caroline Romney

Camilla Eyring

Colonia Juarez, where my grandparents settled, nestled in the rolling foothills of the Sierra Madres. I remember that after a long dusty drive from Dublan to Juarez, through mesquite, sand, and chaparral, one rounded the last hill and descended a dugway into the compact mass of trees in a narrow valley along the Piedras Verdes River. But this was the new town; the colonists had first settled farther down in the open. After investing great effort in building homes and a dam and planting crops, they learned that the land to which they had bought title was upstream. They had to move into the canyon, less than a mile wide.

In 1885 numerous federal prosecutions for unlawful cohabitation were begun in southern Utah. Miles P. Romney, my maternal grandfather, went to Juarez from St. George, Utah, in 1885 with his wife Annie Maria Woodbury. He soon sent for his other wives, Hannah Hill and my grandmother, Catherine Jane Cottam. Grandfather was a skilled carpenter and joiner. He had served as head of all the building trades in St. George and had assisted his father, who was the chief builder of the St. George Temple. In Mexico, Grandfather Romney established a lumberyard and furnished a market for freighters who made regular trips to the sawmill in the mountains. He superintended the building of the schoolhouse, the gristmill, and other public projects as well as private homes. In his spare time he made stools, benches, school desks, tables, cupboards, and other simple furniture. He had great interest in dramatics and acted the chief role in most of the plays presented in the community. He

usually led the parade that marked every celebration as grand marshal, with plumes waving
and sword flashing; it was as though the occasion
were created to give him opportunity to perform.
His eloquence in church meetings and his patri-
otic oratory on Mexican national holidays always
moved his audiences. He also read and recited to
his family, implanting his love of the classics and
reverence for the spoken word.

In 1887 Henry Eyring, my paternal grandfather, also moved to Colonia Juarez from St.
George. He and Grandfather Romney were well
acquainted. Among other things they had been
major supporters of the library established in St.
George. Elder Erastus Snow selected him to
found and operate the Juarez Cooperative Mer-
cantile Institution. "But first," Brother Snow had
told him, "you should become acquainted with the
Spanish language, know the Mexican people,
their laws, and the technicalities of doing business
in their country." To provide an opportunity for
this training, Elder Snow explained, he was being
called as president of the Mexican Mission. On his
way to Mexico City he stayed in Colonia Juarez for
several months, long enough to haul timber from
the mountains to build on the new townsite the
community's first log house and get his wife Deseret settled. He then continued his journey to
Mexico City in July 1887.

With a small missionary force he looked after
Church affairs in Mexico City until late in 1888,
when he returned to Colonia Juarez to begin the
business for which he had originally been
appointed. During the months away he had ac-

quired a knowledge of the Spanish language, become versed in commercial law, learned the details of doing business with Mexican officials and commercial houses, and located the merchandise with which to stock his store. He shipped his $1500 worth of goods to Colonia Juarez, where a neat frame building, equipped with shelves and warehouse space, was ready, and began the long-planned merchandising business. The Co-op operated for the public benefit, materially raising standards of living and bringing prestige to the town.

In 1890 he brought my grandmother, Mary Bommeli, from St. George to join him and Deseret.

Always prompt in meeting his obligations, habitually punctual in beginning his day's work, and painstakingly careful that his books were accurately kept in the Spanish language, he exemplified downright honesty and undeviating integrity, making a lasting impression on the lives of all who knew him. His kindliness to his employees elicited willing service from them. Once when a dishonest customer claimed to have paid the bill he owed, Grandfather simply marked it paid. One of the clerks, unwilling to see Grandfather cheated, overcharged the dishonest customer a little at a time until by careful calculation the debt had been paid, with interest. Grandfather never knew.

My father, Edward Christian Eyring, came to Juarez several years after his father. He had helped his father move, then returned to Arizona to work as a ranch hand. My mother, Caroline

Cottam Romney, came with her parents when she was thirteen years old. When Father was twenty-two and Mother sixteen they met at a ranch near Juarez and were immediately attracted to one another. She soon promised to marry him, but one day when he was on holiday in Casas Grandes with a group of friends, Father had some beer and smoked a cigar. Grandfather Romney heard about it and in a fury told Caroline that she could never speak to Ed Eyring again. An obedient daughter, for two years she sorrowfully had nothing to do with the young man except to see him at dances, but she had made up her mind she would marry him, and turned away several other proposals of marriage. Finally Grandfather Romney relented, and the young couple resumed their courting. In 1893, in company with Father's sister Ida and Ida's fiance, Edward Turley, and with Grandma Eyring as chaperone, they made the long trip by horsedrawn wagon and by train to Salt Lake City, Utah, to be married in the temple there. Thus I, their first child, was born under the covenant.

I was born in a little red brick house on the east side of the Piedras Verdes River, which divided Colonia Juarez in half lengthwise. The river ran along the bottom of our lot, and the bank was very steep. Though usually a narrow stream, during the summer flood season the river often became a roaring torrent and sometimes washed through our corral. The floods always brought down quantities of driftwood, which men and boys drew out with lassos to be used for firewood.

When I was not quite three years old Father

Top, Camilla's birthplace in Colonia Juarez, Chihuahua, Mexico, December 7, 1894. Left, Camilla, age 1.

went on a mission to Germany, the land of his father's birth. He labored there twenty-seven months. He thought he had left his family provided for through money owed him. He had given a man a team on which the man was to make weekly payments to Mother, but the man disappeared with the team. The men who owed Father did not pay, so while Father was gone, Mother suffered great hardships, sometimes being both cold and hungry, but I always had enough. Mother saw to that. She did not tell Father of her problems for fear he would feel obligated to come home. She did sewing and fed four boarders. She rented out her own bed and slept on the floor, even though she was pregnant. She was determined to save enough money to send to Father to keep him on his mission. When Father had been gone about six months, my sister Mary was born. At that time I had whooping cough, and I was sent to stay with my Grandmother Eyring so the new baby would not be exposed. One of my earliest memories is running to the edge of the porch whenever I had to cough and stooping over the edge to vomit.

When Mary was about one month old I was taken home, but I didn't remember Mother, and I cried to go back with Grandmother. Father did not learn that my little sister had been born deaf until he came home when I was just past five. Mother had kept this secret too, so as not to worry him. When he returned I did not know him. I couldn't understand the great fuss Mother was making over the strange man with the beard. I asked her to please send him away. But what a joy it was to her to have Father home again.

Camilla, 7; Mary, 4; Henry, 1

My Romney grandparents had moved to a big farm in Dublan, eighteen miles away. Every three or four weeks we went to visit them and had a grand time. Once Father hitched a span of horses to the two-seat white-topped buggy and we made the trip of eighteen miles in three hours, a record speed.

Of necessity, the people in the colonies were self-sufficient, maintaining themselves with products from their own gardens, farmyard animals, and what manufacturing they could do themselves. Mother made her own soap, which she used to clean everything from faces to floors. Father repaired the family shoes.

Many activities of the home required cooperation of neighbors and friends. Rag bees, sewing bees, and quilting bees brought neighbors together to help and to visit. The hostess traditionally provided a hot meal. At such times old clothes were torn into strips, sewn together, and wound into balls ready to be made into carpets for the parlors. Every spring each rag carpet was taken up, placed over a clothesline, and beaten with a broom until the accumulated dust was removed. The old straw had to be removed from the floor, the floor scrubbed, and a fresh layer of wheat straw spread out. Then the carpet was stretched and tacked into place. We children had fun tromping over the spongy floor and hearing the crunch of the fresh straw.

We went to Sister McDonald's home for yeast. Mother used to put half a cup of sugar or flour in a small bucket, and we children would exchange it for a quantity of hop yeast. I could smack my lips still at the memory of that delicious yeast. The little bucket would be almost full when I left Sister McDonald's, but it was apt to be somewhat less when I reached home, for I kept sipping it along the way, hoping there would be enough left when I reached home for Mother to mix bread.

When I started to school the fall before my eighth birthday, Ada Helquist was my seatmate, and we were inseparable chums. All the seats were double, cumbersome, homemade affairs, and everyone had a seatmate. Sometimes a punishment meted out—for example, for being tardy—

Camilla, 9; Mary, 6; Henry, 3; Edward, 1

was to put a girl with a boy. This was enough to bring anyone to school on time. Elva Gibbons was another early school friend. We had a "post office" in a hollow log out in the school woodpile, and every morning each would deposit a letter for the other in this secret place. The letters were apt to be rather mushy.

Father was always very patient with his chil-

Camilla visits in 1968 the spot on the Piedras Verdes where she was baptized in icy water in December 1904

dren—Mother had to do the disciplining. Father slapped me only once. It was a cold winter day with snow on the ground, unusual for our Mexican climate. He sent me on an errand to the next-door neighbors, the Petersons, and told me to put on a coat. I did the errand but forgot the coat. When I came back he slapped me because I had disobeyed. I took a chair, set it in the corner of the room, and sat with my face to the wall for hours, brokenhearted.

Because my grandparents all lived in plural marriage and had gone to Mexico for that reason, I should probably not have been surprised that Father might also feel impelled to make that commitment. But when, at age eight, I became aware that my father was courting my mother's younger sister Emma, I was jealous for Mother. I first sensed something was happening when I watched Father and Aunt Emma one day bringing the team up the road for our trip home from a visit to my Romney grandparents' farm; they laughed and talked like a courting couple. Later on, when Father had been away and Mother told me that Aunt Emma would be coming to live with us as Father's second wife, I was upset. But she had given her consent, believing as Father did that the only way for them to attain the highest glory in the celestial kingdom was to faithfully live by The Principle. They understood that in Mexico it was still permissible, and they were encouraged in that understanding.

When I was to set the table for dinner, I found the oldest silverware to put at Aunt Emma's place. I feel ashamed now of my petty reaction, but as a child I did not understand the great sacrifice it represented on the part of all three of them to live harmoniously in that relationship. Aunt Emma lived with us for a year until a separate house was constructed for her.

After I had been in the second grade a few months, my teacher told me I could go into the third grade. I cried and cried because I didn't want to leave my friends. Besides, the third grade teacher, Miss Butler, had a reputation for being very strict and cross, and I was afraid of her. The first morning I went into the new class, however, Miss Butler came to me and, putting her arm around me, said, "You've come to be my little girl, have you?" She won my heart at once, and I always thought her a most wonderful teacher.

Augusta Ivins was my new seatmate, and for the next four years we were inseparable bosom companions. Gusta and I used to roam over the

Ida Harper, Zara Bentley, Camilla

hills together hunting pretty rocks, wild flowers, and prickly-pear apples. We confided every secret thought to each other and carved our initials on rocks and in the top branches of trees. We hid a collection of pins and hairpins on the trunk of a thick cypress tree, a secret that we shared with no one. We took turns eating Sunday dinner at each other's home. I once spilled tomato soup all over their white tablecloth and nearly died of shame.

When I went to play at Gusta's house after school, my instructions from Mother were to be home at sundown, not a minute later. Gusta lived at the foot of the hills on the other side of the village, and if I began running as soon as the sun disappeared at her house, I could just get to my

Camilla with Augusta Ivins

home on the east side of the river by the time the sun was down there. If I missed it I got spanked.

When I was thirteen Anthony W. Ivins, our stake president, Gusta's father, was made an apostle and the Ivins family moved to Salt Lake City. This was a tragedy for me. I didn't think I could live without Gusta. How I wept, sure I would never find such a chum again. For years she and I corresponded frequently, and I saw her when I went to Provo to school, but, of course, we had grown apart—though all our lives we have exchanged Christmas cards.

In the fall of 1907 we moved to our new home on the west side of town and of the river. How we hated to move to a new neighborhood. Mother felt funereal about it, but after we settled in we liked it very much.

Among the grade school teachers I remember

well was Brother Haag, a big German. He was
very strict, but he surely knew how to get us to
sing. He had us prepare several operettas. In one,
he took the part of a schoolmaster, and at the end
of the play he was bowing to the audience when
the curtain came down and hit him on the back of
the head. I was terribly embarrassed for him.
After all of his work, it was sad to end the play in
comic fashion. His false teeth didn't fit very well,
and I was often afraid for him, that he would lose
them.

Brother Gonzales, a native Mexican convert to
the Church, who had married one of the colonists'
daughters, was our Spanish teacher. We attended
a class in Spanish every day all through the grades
and used Spanish daily in speaking to the Mex-
icans who lived among us.

Father used to go to El Paso once or twice a
year to buy clothes for us all. He always brought us
loads of presents, and sometimes we went with
him. In the fall of 1904 the family made the trip to
El Paso on the train. While we were there we went
to see the Barnum and Bailey Circus, the wonder
of wonders. The giraffes and the trapeze perfor-
mers most captured my imagination. In El Paso
we stayed in an upstairs hotel room, and to get
water for the washbowl we had to go down an
outside stairway into a patio. The proprietress
kept a wad of tobacco under her lower lip, and
there were tobacco stains down the sides of her
chin. It was a scandalous sight for us children to
see a woman chew tobacco.

Father owned a big cattle ranch and rode the
range all the time. He employed Mexican help,

and members of one tenant family living near us were almost like members of our own family. The man, Chico, was faithful and friendly; he would do anything for Father or for any of us. We liked his wife, Juana, too, but Chico was our favorite.

We always had a fine herd of horses. Father had a huge black Percheron stallion that he kept for breeding purposes. I had a horse of my own, Apache, a dapple gray, and rode with Father sometimes. I had a beautiful side saddle, which father paid a big price for, and I wore a divided skirt of khaki. One day I was riding old Tom, a sorrel pony, at a swift gallop down the main street of town. He shied at a piece of paper that blew under his feet and left me in a heap in the dust, more embarrassed than hurt.

During the summers almost every day groups of young people would go up the river to the edge of town to the old swimming hole. We had never heard of swimming suits, but just wore old dresses. We changed our clothes in the bushes beside the river. Boys and girls went swimming separately. Sometimes when the river was flooded and running swiftly, we would jump in upstream, swim down with the current, and then climb out and walk back up the bank to swim down again.

The summer of 1908 we lived on the ranch eight miles up the river from town. There were a hundred range cows to be milked. Uncle Andrew Eyring made three big cheeses every morning. I helped break and work the curd. One morning when we had cooked whole wheat for breakfast, I took my bowl into the dairy room and skimmed some of the thickest cream into my bowl of wheat.

I enjoyed the gorging, but later when it came back
up, it wasn't so pleasant, and for years I sickened
at the smell of boiling wheat.

Father's older brother, Uncle Henry Eyring,
went blind when he was a young man, before I was
born. He sat in an armchair near the front gate of
Grandmother's house and listened to the foot-
steps of people passing by. He could recognize
their walk and would call out their names in greeting. When I was small he liked to hold me on his
lap. He gave me the little metal stars and horse-
shoes that came on his plug tobacco. The morning
Uncle Henry died Mother came into my bedroom
to tell me. I was grief stricken.

This is the first death I recall clearly. Both my
grandfathers had died when I was young, but my
relationship with them had been fairly formal, so
my feelings were not much affected. At Grandfather Eyring's funeral my main concern was my
new blue felt hat with a white pompom. As we
mourners passed between parallel lines of Church
members I was peeking about to see who would
notice my new hat. Uncle Henry's death, on the
other hand, represented the loss of a companion.
I had a feeling that I had been special to him.

His death left Grandma Eyring living alone, so
it was decided I should go to live with her, just
four blocks away. I lived with her when I was
thirteen and fourteen and in the seventh grade. I
was very fond of Grandmother, but she had some
decided ideas that were hard for a little girl to live
up to. She was absolutely opposed to novel reading, and at that age I had an insatiable appetite for
novels. In my upstairs bedroom was a cupboard

full of books belonging to my cousins Theresa and Beatrice Snow, who had also lived with Grandmother. Every night I went to bed soon after supper, and by the light of a small coal-oil lamp I read until I heard Grandmother start up the stairs; then I quickly extinguished the light and went to sleep. I read all the Horatio Alger series, Louisa May Alcott's books (I related to Jo, the tomboy), and whatever else came to hand.

Grandmother was always up at daylight and went out to work in the flowers or vegetable garden. As soon as I heard her start down the stairs I would begin reading again. She would come in to call me just in time for breakfast. Often she said to me, "Camilla, I don't see how you can sleep so many hours." She never knew of the hours I had been reading.

During the time I lived with Grandmother, I suffered intensely from a fear of insanity. There was a boy in the town who was retarded, and I looked at him with horror and wondered if I would be like that. Every time Mother scolded me for forgetting something or for any other trivial mistake I said to myself, "See, I am going crazy." I was dreadfully morbid and self-conscious, and I didn't dare confide in anyone. Finally I happened to read an article in *American Motherhood* magazine describing this mental condition as common to adolescence. It was like a release from jail to be reassured that other youngsters had the same fears and that I was not peculiar.

Grandmother slept between two deep feather ticks, and every day she beat and plumped them up until they were two or three feet thick. For breakfast she always made either burned crust or bran "coffee" and served it with her delicious white bread and butter, which I liked to sop in it. She made the best bread imaginable. When she took it out of the oven, she wrapped it in a white flannel blanket and let it sweat, which seemed to add to its delectable flavor.

In one of her cupboard drawers she kept several bottles of tiny sugar pills. Their medicinal properties must have been very mild, for I never lost an opportunity to snitch some, and there never seemed to be any ill effects—they tasted like fine-flavored candy to me. Grandmother had a large vineyard, which she cultivated beautifully. The grapes were delicious, especially the Isabellas, dark blue grapes with slippery skins. We ate them fresh, and canned juice and jelly.

The parlor in her home was carefully closed, to be used for company, and we lived in the big kitchen.

Aunt Emma and her family lived in the house next to us, and she and Mother took turns with chores, such as caring for milk and eggs. As the eldest in both families, I was often given responsibility for the children when their mothers were away, so I had plenty of experience at baby tending. Maybe that's why I have never since wanted to tend anyone else's babies.

I helped Mother with the children and the laundry. In those days the dirty diapers were stored in a sack for a week and then washed out in one dirty tubful the night before wash day. That was always my assignment, and it still makes me almost sick to remember the nasty job. Mary, my

sister just younger than I, was my special care, and
since she was deaf, it was sometimes a real responsibility. Mother insisted that I should take her to
parties with me. This was a trial, for many times I
felt she hadn't been invited.

I had some real struggles with my brother
Henry. Once when I was about twelve and Henry
six, he refused to mind some instruction of mine
when I was tending the family in Mother's ab-
sence, so I attempted to put him in the dark closet
under the stairway. He fought desperately, for he
was afraid, but I finally succeeded in forcing him
in. When I let him out he said, "You fool!" In tears
I told him of the punishment the Bible predicted
would come to anyone who used that terrible
word. We both wept for fear perdition was sure.
Hell's fire seemed pretty close that time.

School played an important part in my life.
The eighth grade met in the Academy building,
and we felt like real grown-ups. I was the president of this eighth grade graduating class, and at
the graduation exercises I was to give the wel-
coming address; I had such a cold I couldn't speak
above a whisper. I suffered intensely, sure that
everyone was laughing at me.

About this time a group we called "our crowd"
developed, six girls and six boys who had good
times together. We had picnics, hayrides, candy
pulls, and parties. We were very exclusive and
clannish. The "smart" thing to do was to have
oyster suppers and serve homemade root beer.
These we had quite often. I didn't like the root
beer, and I had such a firm conviction that it was
not quite right to drink "beer" that I would never

Girls of "our crowd" wearing matching dresses: Clessa Walser, Mae Cooke, Lula Romney, Camilla Eyring, Adelia Stowell, Ada Helquist

drink it, so the others always sarcastically made me a glass of lemonade. One night we were having the supper at Elletts' home, and two of us girls went out to the kitchen to open a keg of root beer. When we loosened the cork just a little, the force of the effervescence blew the cork to the ceiling and sprayed root beer all over the kitchen.

At a candy pull at the molasses mill one night the hour was late when the molasses candy was done, so instead of waiting for it to cool, the boys poured it into a bucket of cold water and each one reached a hand in for a piece to pull. While I was trying to get my share, they poured some more boiling candy in, blistering my hand badly.

Father never did approve of the boys in this group, and I always went with them over his protest. Sometimes, when I came home later than I should have, I would take my shoes off and sneak up the stairs to bed. The stairs were sure to squeak

before I could get up to the top step, and Father
would wake up and scold me a bit.

The first night dance I went to, when I was
fourteen years old, was a Valentine costume
dance at the school, and I went decked out in a
full-skirted purple crepe-paper dress I had made.
I didn't do much dancing and I was devastated,
but Mother tried to console me because it was the
first time.

Soon afterwards a neighbor boy I liked invited
me to go to a dancing party with him. I was delighted. This was my first invitation to go out as a
couple. It marked my growing up. But when I
asked Papa if I could go, he disapproved, saying,
"I wouldn't be found dead in a turnip patch with
that boy." I wept a little and said I had already
accepted. Finally Papa let me go this once, with the
promise there would not be a second date with the
fellow. I never did understand Father's objection.

During this year I was so self-conscious about
boys that I would go around the block to keep
from meeting one who had taken me out.

The local Church leaders were very strict
about dancing. No waltzes were allowed, and the
waltz position was taboo. We just took hold of
hands and pranced around. Those who were daring would clasp hands under their chins and get a
rather close hold that way. Every other dance was
a quadrille or square dance, interspersed with a
schottische, polka, or some other. In the quadrille
we used to swing so hard on the corners that I
became almost too dizzy to stand. We danced the
Virginia reel, too, with plenty of vim.

Basket dances were held frequently for fund

raising. Each girl brought a basket lunch and would be taken home by the boy who bought it. One night when the baskets were being auctioned off, my partner, Ernest Haws, bid five dollars for mine. I was greatly flattered. At another dance my basket was bought by a boy I didn't like. When the dance was over I was supposed to let him take me home, but I didn't want to, so I went into the ladies' restroom and hid. He kept waiting in the hall until finally I climbed out the window and ran home.

My first and only automobile ride while we lived in Mexico was in a car that belonged to Uncle Henry Bowman, who lived in Dublan; I thought of him as my rich uncle. I rode several blocks up Main Street at perhaps ten miles per hour, and I stiffened with pride as I felt that the envious eyes of everyone were upon me. People came rushing from their houses to see the wonder go by.

Along with many other colonists, our family went to El Paso when President William Howard Taft came there to meet President Diaz of Mexico. It was an event of great pageantry, with bands and a parade. The meeting of these two presidents had special significance to the colonists, because it symbolized our double loyalty to the United States and to Mexico.

2

By the fall of 1910 Colonia Juarez was at a high level of prosperity and industries flourished. The Co-op had a stock of merchandise valued at ten thousand dollars. Orders were accepted by telephone and deliveries made free of charge. The shoe and harness shop and tannery, operated by the Taylor brothers, manufactured saddles and harnesses. The gristmill ground day and night, supplying a good grade of flour. Homes were well stocked with provisions: preserved fruits and vegetables in pantries, barreled pork, beans, flour, cornmeal and shorts, apples, root vegetables, and squash in cellars. The Pearson Lumber Company ten miles to the south was connected with the border city of El Paso by daily trains.

Colonia Juarez had no saloons, no pool halls, no problem with drunkenness. Smoking was rare, and the drinking of tea and coffee was discouraged. Church leaders visiting the colony were quick to recognize the high level of cultural achievement.

This is the time I started high school. During my two years of high school I took an active part in class and school activities, holding various offices.

Camilla and mandolin

Report card, Juarez Stake Academy

JUAREZ STAKE ACADEMY
GUY C. WILSON, PRINCIPAL

Examination Record of *Camilla Eyring* Class ....

	FIRST SEMESTER				FINAL	SECOND SEMESTER				FINAL
	1st Month	2nd Month	3rd Month	4th Month		1st Month	2nd Month	3rd Month	4th Month	
Theology	a	A	A	A	A	A	A	A	A	A
~~Mathematics~~ *Zoology*						A	A	A	A	A
English *E. Rhet*	A-	A-	A	A	A	A	A	A	A
Psychology	B	A	B	A	A-	A	A	A	A
Botany	A-	A+	A+	A	A				
Home Sciv	B	A-	A	A	A-	A	A	A	A	A
~~Orch~~ *Music*	B	B	B	B+	B+	A	A			
Mex. History						A	A	A	A	A

A 95%, B-85%, C-75%, D-65%, E- Failure   To Graduate, three-fourths must be C or above

I managed straight A grades both years except for one-fourth unit in string orchestra, where I played a mandolin and got a B. During these two years I read an unconscionable number of novels. I often sat on the back seat in Guy C. Wilson's psychology class reading a novel while we were supposed to recite on psychology.

I took a course in biology under Mr. Oberhansley just at the time when the theory of evolution was a point of great concern. As most adolescent youngsters do, I swallowed the daring new theory hook, line, and sinker, and delighted in arguing with Father and Mother, insisting that I believed profoundly in evolution.

From the time I was fifteen years old I taught a Primary and a Sunday School class, the latter with Theadosia Meacham and Jennie Whipple. I got a feeling I would like to be a "real" teacher someday.

Rumbles of a revolutionary storm had been heard in the colonies for some time, but little attention was paid to them. Porfirio Diaz, the first president of Mexico to give a semblance of peace to the nation, had overstayed his term of office. Everywhere the rich people in fine clothing looked down upon the peons who lived in dire poverty. In the October 1910 election, Madero sought to be elected president of Mexico on a platform to improve the lot of the peons, but he was promptly put in prison by Diaz's men, and it was announced that Diaz had been elected for his seventh term of office.

Madero escaped from jail and promptly denounced Diaz's claim of election. He began to stir up revolution, and the state of Chihuahua, where we lived, with the city of Casas Grandes as the focal point, was the first state to revolt. In the colonies by 1911 the rebels demanded horses, saddles, and food from the colonists, paying with worthless receipts, and they stole anything they could get their hands on. Father lost dozens of head of cattle and horses. We lived in dread. The colonists tried to remain completely neutral, on advice of Elder Ivins, who came to confer with our leaders. However, conditions worsened to the extent that law broke down. Competing rebel bands threatened life and confiscated property. In July 1912 Salazar demanded that the colonists give up their arms. They were unwilling to leave their families wholly unprotected, so the stake president, my uncle Junius Romney, decided that the women and children should move temporarily to the United States for safety.

That summer we had raised lots of blackberries. On Saturday Mother, with our help, canned one hundred quarts of berries. That evening Father came home with word that our guns were to be delivered up to the rebels at the bandstand on Sunday and that the stake leaders had decided we should leave for El Paso immediately. He took up the porch floor and we stored the newly bottled berries underneath, thinking we would soon return to reclaim them. We hid valuables in all the unlikely places we could think of.

We were allowed to take just one trunk of clothes for Father's family of thirteen. I wanted so much to put in my doll and some other treasures, but there was no room. I had always been a great collector and had kept all my school papers, letters, toys—everything I had ever owned; now I had to leave them all, never to see them again.

In the morning Father drove us to Pearson in the white-topped buggy. This railroad station was

Spencer and Camilla visit in 1968 the Eyring home in Juarez, where the family lived between 1907 and the exodus in 1912. Camilla's room was behind front dormer window.

about eight miles from Juarez. There were dozens of buggies and wagons and crowds of refugees waiting for the train to carry us to the safety of the United States. Grandmother Eyring had been robbed of forty dollars that morning by a rebel who invaded her house and demanded her money. A troop of rebels on horseback with guns and bayonets was drawn up in formation at the train station. As one old lady walked by, a soldier hooked his rifle through her handbag and took possession of it. She dared not protest, but went on to the train. A drunken man rode his horse at my sister Isabel, just three, and nearly trampled her, laughing at her fright.

When the last wagon had unloaded on the depot platform at Pearson, several hundred women, children, and elderly persons, assisted by

Scene at the Pearson station as the Saints flee Mexico

a few able-bodied men, were ready to take the
train for El Paso. At Dublan more people crowded
on, making about one thousand refugees packed
onto one train. Our family was in a third-class car
with long, hard benches running lengthwise of
the cars and children and baggage piled on top of
one another. Buggies and wagons were left standing empty at the station. When passenger cars
filled up, boxcars and even a few cattle cars were
attached. Some cars were so crowded that even
standing room was a premium. We all suffered
intensely as the delayed train finally moved off in
the stifling July heat.

The trip to the border at El Paso was only
about 150 miles, but the train went at a snail's pace
and stopped every few miles. We were in terror all
the time lest the rebels waylay us. We traveled all
day and all night. Finally, just as dawn was break-

ing, we crawled slowly across the Rio Grande and were greeted by the sight of the Stars and Stripes. A great shout went up from all the refugees. That sight brought a thrill that is revived in me every time I return to the United States and see the flag again. After a harrowing experience we felt safe once more.

The kind people of El Paso met us at the depot and took us in automobiles (only the second time I'd ridden in one) out to a big lumberyard, where they improvised shelter for the refugees. Hundreds had already arrived before us and hundreds were yet to come. They put us into a huge corral with dust a foot deep, flies swarming, noisy, stinking, and crowded with a mass of humanity. It was enough to make the stoutest heart sink. Those in charge tried to arrange a stall for each family, and we piled in for the night, hanging up blankets in an attempt at a little privacy. During that night five babies were born in these rude shelters.

We felt humiliated as newspaper photographers and reporters recorded our pitiful dependence and as the curious townspeople gawked and pointed at us, as they would animals in a zoo.

Mother had a little money, so the next day she scurried around to find us lodgings that were a little more private. She was expecting her ninth child in a few months. She finally took one room in a small hotel for the fourteen of us: Mother and her seven children, her younger sister Emma, who was also Father's second wife, Aunt Emma's four children, and Grandma Eyring. It was an inside room at that—no outside ventilation in that hot July weather. There was just room to spread quilts all over the floor, and we managed to be one deep at least until we were asleep. Some of us slept under Grandma's bed. In this room we ate our meals as well as slept. In the morning I took the children out to play in the fresh air.

We expected Father would come out of Mexico at any time to get us, so we stayed there about a week. We then moved to a tenement way down on Talles Street near the Rio Grande. There we had two rooms and at least some fresh air and a place to get outdoors. Families in six or eight apartments shared one kitchen, so the women took turns cooking for the crowd. The government sent men around every morning with daily rations. They brought white baker's bread, puffed wheat and rice, milk, and canned salmon. I suppose there were other things, but that is the diet I remember.

There was no furniture in the tenement. Our one trunk had a flat top, so we used it for a table, all sitting on the floor around it. During the day the bedding was rolled up around the sides of the room, and we sat on the rolls. I was embroidering a set of lingerie, so I spent many hours sitting on the rolls and doing my needlework.

I begged Mother to let me get a job. Many of the girls were going out to work in homes, and finally I persuaded her. I got work as a maid with a well-to-do family. I was the first-floor maid, with a white cap and apron; I answered the door, waited table, scoured the silver every Thursday morning, and in the afternoon took two spoiled youngsters to the park. For my services I earned four dollars a week—and was very proud of the earnings.

Tenement on Talles Street, El Paso, provided temporary housing for six families, who shared single kitchen

While we were getting settled in El Paso, affairs took a decidedly serious turn in Colonia Juarez. The looting and threats of the rebels increased, and President Romney decided that the men should leave to join their families in El Paso, since there seemed no chance of protecting their homes from looting without bloodshed. Uncle Junius went through great anguish because there was dissension about the move; a substantial minority of the people felt they might not have had to leave had matters been handled differently. Most agreed, however, that to stay might result in bloodshed, and they were willing to abandon their property, at least for a time, rather than take that chance.

In the tithing office were hidden about a hundred new guns that had not been turned over to the rebels. Rather than have them discovered and increase hostility, the leaders appointed Father and his brother-in-law, Miles Romney, to get the guns out. The rebels were camped near the building, and the two men pulled a board off the high fence and slipped the rifles, packed in cases of about six each, through the fence and onto the backs of horses. They cached the guns in a cave several miles away in an all-night effort. The men then came across the border five days by horseback, bringing with them three hundred guns and five hundred horses. They displayed a white flag to show their peaceful intentions. Across the border they were nearly fired on by Americans who thought they were rebels carrying the white flag as a ruse. Father finally joined us after we had been in El Paso about two weeks.

Father did not much like my working as a maid, and word came that we would likely be able to return to Mexico soon, so I gave up my job. The man for whom I worked was a railroad official, and he gave me a pass on the railroad back to Juarez, but I never got a chance to use it.

Disappointment came—more trouble in the colonies—and we were not allowed to return yet. I got another job in a home near the fairly decent house Father had rented for our family in Highland Park. I cared for a sick woman and her husband. I had stayed there for a few weeks when it became clear that it would be some time before we could go home, if ever.

Several times Father returned to Mexico to try to ship some of his cattle out, but he never succeeded. He finally had to abandon virtually everything we owned. It is hard to imagine the disappointment he felt in losing his ranch, cattle, horses, and homes, all left to despoilers, but he turned to the task at hand, of reestablishing himself and providing for his family of fifteen—himself, Mother and her eight children, and Aunt Emma and her four children.

The railroads offered free transportation to the refugees who wanted to seek homes away from the border. My parents and I decided that I should go, alone, to Utah to finish high school and try to make my own way.

My uncle Carl Eyring had offered me a place to stay in Provo, Utah, and I appreciated the opportunity. It meant setting out on a great adventure. At the same time I was filled with anxiety; I had been suddenly precipitated from a small, sheltered community surrounded by family into a large world offering me no security.

I was seventeen.

3

Taking advantage of the railroad's offer, Camilla left El Paso for Provo, Utah, on the first of September, 1912. Mary had been sent with friends to Ogden, Utah, to the School for the Deaf. Other people from the Colonies were also on the train, but Camilla preferred to try to make her own way without relying on them. When they left El Paso it was still very hot. As the train passed through the mountains of Colorado it began to snow and grew bitterly cold, but her coat was packed away in her trunk. She had a pair of cotton blankets in a roll that she was carrying with her, but she was too proud to wrap herself in them until it came to the point of freezing. When she finally used them, to her embarrassment she heard a woman say, "Well, she finally has sense enough to wrap up."

In Provo it was bitter cold and raining, and there was no one at the depot to meet her. She had never felt more bereft and lonely. A Sister Taylor, who also got off the train in Provo, kindly helped Camilla get to her uncle Carl Eyring's home, where she had been invited to live. The small house already held Carl and his sister Fern, who were only a few years older than Camilla, and their widowed mother, Aunt Deseret.

They were generous enough to take me in to work for my board. To begin with I felt like, and

36

probably was, a charity ward. I scarcely dared to eat as much as I wanted. The change of climate made me ravenously hungry, and I never felt satisfied. Our diet consisted of boiled wheat flakes, served with skim milk, for breakfast; mashed potatoes thinned with water, and white beans seasoned with cooking fat, for dinner; and bread with a little milk for supper. I shared a room with Fern. They were very kind to take me in, but they were all three very set in their ways. They never went out at night, and there was no fun or life about the place. When I later started going out, I tried to meet my dates at the door and rush away. For entertainment we went dancing or to parties or walked around or sat on an old hayrack on the other side of the block. When I came in after they were all in bed, I felt censured for disturbing them, and they no doubt felt annoyed with me.

Carl was courting Fern Chipman, a popular young lady. She had difficulty choosing between him and another young man who had proposed marriage. About the first of November she told both of them that she had decided not to go out with either of them until she had made up her mind; at Thanksgiving time she would give her answer. I felt so anxious and sorry for Carl. He would go to the back of the lot and pace up and down endlessly, waiting for the time to pass. The tension built higher and higher. Finally, on Thanksgiving, Fern invited Carl to dinner with her family. There could have been no happier Thanksgiving anywhere than in his little house that day. We all rejoiced for him.

When she first arrived in Provo Camilla found work for two weeks packing peaches and earned a few dollars. She needed them, for her parents had little cash, having left everything in Mexico. Her father had a large family and no work, so the family could not support her.

To add to her sad predicament, Camilla's clothes, which her mother had so painstakingly made for her in El Paso, were all wrong. The skirts were up to her knees, and in Provo the girls and women were wearing skirts long. Her dresses were all cotton—and everyone in Provo was wearing wool during the cold winter months. Clothes meant a lot to her, so she suffered agonies over her wardrobe. At first she refused to go to Sunday School, parties, or anywhere except classes because she felt she didn't have suitable clothes. All her dresses had been made by one pattern, with only slight variations. But she soon adjusted to the situation and made the best of it.

Just before Christmas a package came from home, and Camilla opened it immediately. It was a party dress that she needed badly and had asked for, but to her sorrow it was tan, and she wanted pink or blue. And it was made by that same old pattern! Camilla was taking sewing classes in school, so she ripped the dress to pieces, remade it, trimmed it with blue fur, and finally felt she could wear it. Her mother, out of the goodness of her heart, sent Camilla little trinkets, but Camilla had no use for them and thought, "Oh, if Mother would just send me the money instead!"

Camilla's childhood chum, Augusta Ivins, came down from Salt Lake City to see her. The pleasure of the visit was diluted by the fact that Augusta dressed in the latest style; Camilla felt like a backwoods friend.

*Camilla, 18, and Mary, 14, attending
school in Utah*

She suffered so greatly with an inferiority complex
that she made few friends. Her withdrawn disposition
made the experience more miserable than it need have
been. She did well in her studies, though, and made
excellent grades, which compensated somewhat.

That Christmas Camilla went to Salt Lake City and
Mary came from Ogden to join her. They spent a few
days visiting their father's sister, Aunt Millie, and Aunt
Millie's daughter, Beatrice. Camilla again felt like a
charity case and imagined that she and Mary were not
wanted, which made her miserable.

At the Brigham Young Academy the girls' organization had a roller skating party that year and
Camilla went. She crept gingerly around the edge of

the floor, holding tightly to the railing. About every yard her feet went out from under her and she fell, wiping a swath of the floor. Each time she dragged herself up and tried again. She was wearing her new winter coat and ripped the sleeve partly out. The next morning she was so stiff and sore that she could scarcely get out of bed. Later she had similar experiences with ice skating and with trying to learn to ride a bicycle. She concluded that she had no sense of balance when not standing on the ground.

During the summer of 1913 Camilla and Mary did not have the money to go home to Arizona, where their father had rented a farm and located his two families. Mrs. Ida Stewart Peay, an old friend of their mother and an invalid for fifteen years, offered the girls a home for the summer with free board and room. Mary was touchy and easily hurt when people laughed and did not tell her why, or failed to communicate the gist of the conversation. Camilla spent much of the time trying to calm those troubled waters. Besides providing board and room, Mrs. Peay paid Camilla two dollars and fifty cents a week for doing her washing and ironing and keeping the house clean. Camilla knew "Aunt Ida" could ill afford to pay her anything; Mr. Peay was a blacksmith and they had only enough to get by on. It was just out of the goodness of her heart that she took the girls in.

She was the grandest person I have ever known. There she lay flat on her back, but every morning she dressed herself neatly and carefully. She wore trim little black slippers and pretty print dresses, and looked like a picture as she lay on her bed. All around her bed she had bags and pockets

Camilla, age 19

with things she needed. She made her daughter Anna's dresses by hand, did all her darning and patching, and, when we were not there, did much of the food preparation—even mixing cakes—and then had her husband or children put the food on the stove to cook. Besides all this, she had a portable typewriter that she placed on top of herself, and she wrote stories and articles that were printed in magazines. She was always jolly and full of fun, and her home was one place in which I honestly felt welcome. I loved her devotedly.

About this time Camilla received a telegram from

BRIGHAM YOUNG UNIVERSITY 1912-13

MONTHLY REPORT OF

Camilla E. Young ......of Art & Man. Train Dept.

STUDIES	Units	1st MO.	2nd MO.	3rd MO.	4th MO.	1st SEM.	5th MO.	6th MO.	7th MO.	8th MO.	2nd SEM.
Theology *e*	½	a a	a+a		a+a	a+a	a a				
English *History* *E*	1	B+	B+ a	a		a a	a B a				
Design .... ./........	½										
Studio..............	¼										
Woodwork..........	½										
Draughting	½										
Dressmaking	¾										
Domestic Science *c*	1	a a	a a		a a	a a a					
Domestic *Science*	1	a B+	a a		a a a	a a					
...." ... *Art c*	1	B+	B B+	a		a a a a					

☞ A Duplicate of this Card will cost 25 cents   [OVER]

Report card from Brigham Young University, 1912-13, including college credits in home economics

her father: "NO LETTER FOR WEEK. MOTHER MUCH WORRIED. IF ANYTHING WRONG WIRE IMMEDI-ATELY." Camilla had not written because at the moment she did not have the price of a two-cent stamp.

Besides working for the Peay family, Camilla washed for another woman and ironed for still another, so at times her total weekly income was four and a half dollars. The school year 1913-14 was to be Camilla's senior year in high school, and in addition to taking enough classes to graduate, she took several college courses in home economics, enough to major in this department. She hoped to get a job teaching home economics the next year.

Fortunately for her, the school passed a ruling that spring that the girls' graduation dresses should not cost over three dollars. Camilla was taking sewing in school, so she made a fine white dress with yards and

Left, graduation from high school, 1914. Right, Camilla in dress she made for graduation at cost of $3.00.

yards of insertion and lace. She was really proud of it (and for the rest of her life kept it carefully packed away). She made herself several dresses that year in school and felt less self-conscious because now her clothes looked more like those of the other girls.

There were many firsts. At home she had never been allowed to "round dance" or take a waltz position; dance partners were permitted only to hold hands. But at the dances in Provo things were somewhat more relaxed.

> The first time I went onto the dance floor in Provo and the boy put his arm around me in waltz position, I was so shocked I wasn't sure I hadn't been morally assaulted. What a sheltered life I had led! But there was always a dance manager

walking the floor, and if he saw a couple getting too close together, he would tap them on the shoulder and remind them that there must always be space between them.

Walter Cottam, a cousin who lived in St. George, was a special friend of Camilla's that year, and they had many good times together, long walks and talks. One night they started to walk to the huge "Y" high on the mountainside and it was nearly morning when they got back.

Camilla saw her first motion picture in Provo.

In our childhood it was a thrill to be able to look through the glasses of a stereopticon viewer and see the pictures take depth. Father had brought many pictures from Germany when he returned from his mission, scenes of the Rhine River and the torture chamber where prisoners had been punished. I took lots of still pictures with a little box camera I had brought from Mexico, but now I saw a real moving picture, such as I had only heard of before. It was a marvel of marvels.

Her second year of school ended satisfactorily, and Camilla was elated that now she could hope to get an honest-to-goodness job! In the spring she applied for a position teaching home economics at Millard Academy in Hinckley, Utah, where her cousin Beatrice Snow had taught. Brother Stevens, the principal, wrote her to meet him in Springville, where the Academy's basketball team was scheduled to play. She was fearful at meeting a possible employer, but she landed the job and finally had the prospect of being fully independent.

Camilla and her mother in summer of 1914, Thatcher, Arizona. This was Camilla's first reunion with her family since the flight from Mexico.

Now, after two years away from her parents, she was to go home for the summer to visit and make outlines for the next winter's teaching. The family had moved to Thatcher, Arizona, and were living in an old school building. Her father had a livery stable and also carried the mail from the depot to the post office. Of the six children at home, Rose, who had been born after Camilla left El Paso, was a year and a half old, and Joseph, who had been a baby, was a little cotton-top fellow nearly four years old.

Camilla was delighted to be home. Soon after she arrived her mother insisted she go with her to visit "Grandma" Fife, and there she met Iretta and Caroline Layton. Iretta took her under her wing at once, and they became good friends. She took Camilla into her "crowd," and many of the friendships Camilla developed there were to last through the years.

Her mother, anxious for Camilla to have a good time, made arrangements with a friend for the friend's son to come and take Camilla to a dance in the cultural hall of the ward. Though Camilla remonstrated, her mother insisted, so she got ready and waited, but the boy did not show up. Finally she went to the dance with her girl friends and had a wonderful time. The boy was there also, but he did not dance with Camilla—and he never did make any explanation. She was puzzled, but not sad.

One night Iretta and Camilla went to a picture show in the old Woods showhouse. Afterwards they went to a dance and then home with Ray Killian and Bill McRae. Camilla was to stay with Iretta. Soon after they went to bed Camilla was awakened by Iretta's screams, and she felt someone grab her shoulders. Hearing the screams, "Aunt Cynthia" Layton, who was sleeping in the next room, grabbed her pistol and shot through the door at the intruder, who ran down the lane, jumped into a buggy, and drove away quickly. The girls were so frightened they did not dare go to bed again, but sat shivering with a gun ready until daylight, when they notified the sheriff. The officers made a search and questioned the girls, but could not discover who the intruder was. The girls remembered a boy who watched them closely at the show the night before, so the officers questioned him, but the investigation proved inconclusive.

*Left, Camilla and Iretta
Layton in summer of 1914
at Mt. Graham, Arizona.
Below, Camilla with
friends at the lumber flume.*

With friends on way to picnic, summer 1914

The young people had many good times that summer. On July 24 they went in a buggy up to the flume at the foot of Mount Graham for a picnic. The flume carried lumber from the sawmill at the top of the mountain in a stream of water down the steep mountainside to a lumber yard. They donned overalls and sat on a board in the swift stream and careened down the flume. It seemed wickedly dangerous.

Camilla was the new girl in the community, and Bill McRae was the boy who gave all the new girls a fling.

He worked in the bank and had a rubber-tired buggy
and fast horse, so she felt rather flattered when he
squired her around for a while. LeRoi C. Snow had a
private little dance hall, and the young people had
some nice parties there. For one party Camilla volun-
teered to make lemon pie. She had been hired as a
cooking teacher and was expected to know how to
cook, but the recipe she used was for lemon cake
filling, and the pie turned out to be embarrassingly
sticky.

Near the end of the summer Spencer Kimball, who
had been working at a dairy in Globe and who was
Iretta's good friend, came to Thatcher for one of the
dances at Snow's before he left on a mission. They
were introduced, but he didn't dance with Camilla.
She felt disappointed.

When fall came she set out by train for Hinckley,
Utah. It was midnight when she arrived at Oasis, the
railroad station closest to Hinckley. Just the old
stationmaster was at the depot, and he took her to a
little old hotel across the track, led her up the stairs by
the light of his lantern, and lighted a coal-oil lamp in
the bedroom for her. Her imagination ran rampant,
about lone, defenseless girls being waylaid, and she
had had the unnerving experience at Iretta's home.
That night she was so frightened she could scarcely
stand up. As soon as the old man was out the door she
closed it quickly and bolted it. She slept very little
during what was left of the night, starting at every
creak of the old building.

In the morning she rode the eight miles to Hinck-
ley with the mailman in his buckboard and went to the
Wright home, where she was to board for the winter.
Her room, a small one on the north side of the second

Teaching Domestic Science A at Milford Stake Academy, Hinckley, Utah

floor, had a single window, a bed, table, small stove, and dresser. She was quite comfortable but also quite lonely, starting again in a new community at age nineteen and expecting to be a teacher.

Camilla taught cooking, sewing, and embroidery. She enjoyed the association with young people, many of whom were her age. She enjoyed especially earning seventy-five dollars a month and the independence it represented. She always worried about her adequacy as a teacher, but she learned a great deal from her class preparation and from trying to teach others.

After Christmas a special friend returned from his mission and started school at the Academy. He was good looking and interesting, and he and Camilla became very close friends. They had a falling out when another fellow became flirtatious and he thought she responded a little too much to the attention, but later they patched up their differences and resumed their dating.

Camilla and Ella Hafen at beach in California, summer 1915

In the spring of 1915 Camilla decided to attend the University of California at Berkeley for a summer session. She had saved nearly enough money, and her uncle Junius Romney went with her to the Farmers and Merchants Bank, where she secured a fifty-dollar loan with his guarantee. Mary Merkley, Mae Mortensen, Charles McClelland, her uncle Thomas Romney, and she all boarded at the same home in Berkeley. The International Exposition was in full swing in San Francisco that summer, and they went several times, crossing the bay by ferry.

Camilla's sister Catherine recalls, "I received in the mail a small card, the shape and color of a cucumber, from my big sister, Camilla, when she was away studying at Berkeley. I carried it around with me for weeks, and when I married it was still among my treasures. Camilla had picked up the card, which advertised dill pickles, at the World's Fair, and she had thoughtfully sent one to each of her little sisters."

That fall Camilla returned to the Wrights', but this time she had as a roommate the new English teacher, Beth Cook. Two other teachers were also boarding at the Wright home. The four women decided to move into their own bachelor quarters. They found a small house available nearby and broke the news to Mrs. Wright, who did not like the idea of losing all four boarders, but they were determined that they could be more comfortable and live more cheaply on their own.

The young women called their new quarters "Cozy Cottage." Beth had a way with men, so the girls straightway had lots of company and many good times. Camilla's special friend was attending school in Provo, but she had many opportunities to date other young men. Then she learned that her friend was to be married to a young woman he had met on his mission. Camilla had been very fond of him and felt disappointed and angry at being jilted. He came to Hinckley one weekend to have a talk with her but she

Left, skating with Parley Roper. Below, horseback riding. Bottom, riding motorcycle near Hinckley, Utah, 1915.

Above, shooting a gun.
Left, boating with friends.

was not there—she had gone on a motorcycle to a picnic with another young man to avoid him. She figured he was coming to make an explanation, and she did not want to hear it. That was the end of that romance.

CAMILLA EYRING.

Domestic Science.

B. Y. U. 1912-14.
U. of California Summer Session 1915.
Teacher in Millard Academy 1914-15.

Faculty picture in Milford Stake Academy yearbook, 1916

After being away from home two years, Camilla teaching in Hinckley and Mary in the School for the Deaf in Ogden, Utah, Mary and Camilla were to go home for the summer. They went on the train, which took them by way of Los Angeles. There they stayed overnight at the Rosslyn Hotel, where they had a beautiful room. But Camilla was shocked the next day when she had to pay the six-dollar bill, two or three times what she expected to pay. She had forgotten to ask the price of the room.

That summer Camilla's father bought a farm in Pima and moved the families to a two-room frame house on the mesquite-covered hill until more room could be made. Temporarily Aunt Emma's family lived in tents. Though she enjoyed the visit, Camilla did not like living with two families in such crowded, primitive conditions. The only water was a tap in the yard. But she had to endure it for only a few weeks until she was off again, this time to Logan, Utah, to attend Utah Agricultural College with money she had saved. She had a nice suit, with hat and shoes to match, to wear as she left for this new school, and this bolstered her self-confidence.

At college in the fall Carrie Leigh was assigned as her roommate, and they soon got eight girls together to rent a house. They divided into pairs and took turns with the household chores. Though they didn't always get along well together, they managed to have some good times and to entertain a great deal. They were all scraping by financially; Camilla corrected papers for twenty-five cents an hour to supplement her savings.

About midyear Camilla was pledged to Sigma Theta Phi sorority. Marguerite Cannon, whom she had known in Mexico, sponsored her. The pledge period lasted long, and Camilla had to spend considerable time at the sorority house, cleaning, darning the girls' socks, and doing other chores. The pledges had to put on a "funny-paper show" and the sorority members showered them with peanut shells. What a mess the house was in—but what a sense of belonging the girls each had! For Camilla it was especially rewarding, for she enjoyed the comradeship that membership in the sorority gave her; no one snubbed her. This helped her overcome her painful shyness.

That winter was the coldest in many years, and everyone had to travel on foot or in sleighs. The stu-

*Left, Camilla chops
kindling, with Carrie
Leigh, Logan, 1917.
Below, Sigma Theta Phi
house at Utah State
University, winter 1917.*

dents had a wonderful time sliding down College Hill
on sleds. The girls lived two blocks west of town, about
a mile from campus. Every morning they would bun-
dle up in wool caps, fur muffs, and sturdy overshoes

for the hike to school, but by the time they arrived they would have icicles dangling from their caps and on their eyelashes. Many mornings they had to break the trail up the street before the snowplow came along. They might have ridden the streetcar the long way around, but they couldn't afford the five-cent fare.

In the summer of 1917 Camilla worked in Salt Lake City to earn enough money for her train ticket to Arizona, where she had a teaching position at Gila Academy for the fall. She secured a job in a home doing the cooking and general housework, at a wage of five dollars a week. She was extremely proud and did not want any of her friends to know she was a servant. Augusta Ivins did not know; when she got married that summer Camilla crocheted lovely lace inserts for a sheet and pillow slips for her. In June when her friend Iretta came to Salt Lake City to be married, Camilla painted a glowing picture of her occupation: "I am getting practical experience for my work of teaching home economics." What she said was technically true, but it was surely not the reason she worked. Iretta and her fiance took Camilla to a violin recital at the old Salt Lake Theater, which was her only commercial entertainment that summer.

Finally Camilla had enough money for her ticket, and in August she was able to go home. Her family delighted in having Camilla home at last. Except for two visits, she had been away from the family for five years. The younger siblings had always looked to her as a role model. Her going away from home to seek an education inspired the younger brothers and sisters to set their goals high for obtaining good educations and preparing for professions. Though the smallest ones scarcely remembered her, she had always been

Camilla with younger sisters: Mary,
standing; Caroline, Isabel, Ruth

thoughtful of them and remembered their birthdays
with a little letter and, if possible, a dime. Her brother
Joseph shyly hid behind his mother's skirts, but Camilla coaxed him into the open and won his heart.

Her sister Rose, who was about five when Camilla
returned to the farm, had rather long hair. Camilla
thought she would look much better with a "Dutch
bob" and offered Rose six cents if she would let it be
cut. Rose was fearful of the haircut, but she could not
resist the bribe. She wore bangs for the next twelve
years, thanks to Camilla.

Camilla had two weeks before she began her next
teaching job, this time at the Gila Academy in Thatch-

er, just six miles from her parents' home in Pima. She would be able to live with her family during the school year and commute by bus to Thatcher.

She hoped to marry, but she was nearly twenty-three in a time when most women married earlier, and she had no intention of marrying just anyone. She had intelligence and energy and a plan. She intended to become a hospital dietician and planned to teach only until she could save enough money to attend Johns Hopkins University, which had the reputation of being best in her field.

4

One evening soon after school began, I had stayed at school for a faculty meeting and was standing on Thatcher's Main Street, waiting for the jitney bus, when Spencer Kimball came along. He introduced himself and said he was going by bus to Pima to visit a friend. We sat together on the bus and discussed Shakespeare and similar high-brow subjects, each hoping to impress the other. I was wearing a white voile dress with blue design. I had made the dress over and wished I were wearing something nicer. He wore white socks, but I forgave him. In Pima he walked me home from the bus and asked if he might call on me sometime. That weekend he invited me to his sister Helen's birthday party, but I had to go to Duncan on a Sunday School stake board visit and couldn't go with him.

One evening a few days later, when I had my hair up in curlers and was in a kimono, getting ready to go to Layton Hall to a dance with Pima friends, here came Mr. Kimball. I had told him he could call me, but had given him no special time. I was in a pickle. I visited with him out on the porch, thinking he might stay only a short time, but it

became apparent that he had come to spend the
evening! I finally told him a crowd of us were
going to the dance, and asked if he'd like to come
along. He seemed delighted, so I rushed to get
ready, and when the car arrived, I went out to ask
my date if this new friend could go along. It really
was a very embarrassing situation. My date was
very put out, and I couldn't blame him. All the

Camilla with friends, October 1917, when Spencer was at BYU

way to the dance he drove as if the devil was after
him. He didn't dance with me once. I felt terribly
guilty; I had played a shabby trick.

Anyway, I tried to make the most of the new
friendship, and when Spencer left about two
weeks later for school in Provo, I sent him my

picture and he carried it in his watch. I was very much in love.

One week after he registered at Brigham Young University, he received notice from his draft board to return home for military service. He arrived home on October 14, 1917. I stayed in Thatcher that day with Jessie Bird so I could see him sooner. From that night our intensive court-ship began. He had nothing special to do, just waiting for the draft call. His father and step-mother had gone east to a convention, leaving a new Chevrolet, so he took me home from school and spent every evening with me from that night until we were married. The evenings were usually rather long, lasting until one or two in the morn-ing. Then I had to teach school all day, while he could sleep in before another evening. I wonder that I didn't lose my job, for I actually went to sleep in school sometimes. The girls in my class knew of the romance and giggled when they looked out the window and saw Spencer in his car waiting to take me home.

Camilla's family all loved Spencer. Her mother courted him with cream pies, her father approved, and the younger children were especially excited about her courtship. Once when Spencer had come to Pima to see Camilla and they were parked in the lane, Rose, young and curious, went out to investigate. Spencer invited her to get in the car with them, put her on his lap and taught her the laughing song, "I Saw a Little Elfman." Camilla was unhappy about the snoop-ing.

They spent a lot of time down at the wooden gate at

*Camilla and Spencer courting in his father's
new Chevrolet, November 1917*

the entrance to the farm lane in happy conversation.
With so many younger children in the family, it was
hard to find a place where they could find relative
privacy.

One weekend we went with another couple to
Roosevelt Dam, a real distance to go in those days.
The car could hardly make the grade over some of
the hills. It was a romantic trip.

One Sunday I fixed dinner for some friends
and Spencer and me. I baked chicken and
brought it to the table all garnished. Then I
attempted to carve it at the table. My knife was
dull and the chicken not too tender, so I could
hardly saw it apart. The dinner was to be a
farewell party for Spencer, since he was to leave
for the army, and I used little flags for decoration.

In the next day or two word came that the next contingent of the draft would not leave for some time, so our intensive courtship continued until we decided we would like to get married before Spencer left. It was a rather momentous decision to make, and I think we both sensed the responsibility. Spencer talked to Father about it. I went to the principal of my school to see if it would be all right, and he said yes, so long as it didn't interfere with my job. That meant there was not enough time to travel to Utah to be sealed in the temple, which was a great disappointment.

It was a local custom to shivaree newly married couples, and since we both disliked this custom very much, we decided to have a quiet wedding and avoid it.

The date was set for November 16. Spencer had thought his father would be home at that time, since he would be returning from an extended trip east, but his father had to go to Phoenix to a state commission meeting, so we decided to go ahead without him.

Spencer's sisters Alice and Helen had offered to give me a bridal shower, but I refused, both because in my pride I did not want anyone to feel obliged to give me anything and because we wanted to keep our marriage plans a secret.

Friday afternoon we went to Safford to get the license. We were fearful someone would see us and suspect what was happening, but they didn't. Spencer had just six dollars in his pocket and no job. The license cost two dollars and fifty cents, so he had three dollars and fifty cents left when we were married.

I went home to get ready, and he was to come with his stepmother, "Aunt Josie," and his sister Helen at seven o'clock. When I got home and began to realize the gravity of the step I was about to take, I was ready to back out. I went into the bedroom and cried and cried. I had ambitions to be a hospital dietician; Spencer had no job and was about to go off to a war from which he might not return; and I was terribly naive about sex. Yet I also loved him desperately and decided I was willing to go ahead despite my fears.

Our old house was such a wreck that I could hardly stand the thought of having Sister Kimball see it. The paper that lined the living room was ragged in places. We gathered tree branches and, in the guise of decoration, covered the worst of the holes. Mother did her best to make things attractive and pleasant, but it was November so there were no flowers. I had no bouquet. We had a piano but no music. Bishop Merrill was to perform the ceremony at eight o'clock.

Spencer told me afterwards that he was so excited that when he went to get into the tub he found he had forgotten to bring the hot water, so he had to call to "Aunt Josie" to bring him the water.

I had insisted that all the little children be put in bed. Just the two boys, Henry, sixteen, and Ed, fourteen, were allowed to remain up. As we waited, I was sitting on Spencer's lap and Henry came into the room and saw us. Flustered and embarrassed, he blurted out, "I'll be as silent as the tomb." That provided some comic relief.

Finally the hour came. We stood together in

*Spencer, 22, and Camilla, 22, married November 16, 1917, Pima,
Arizona*

the living room, just the few family members present with my younger sisters peeking around the corner. Spencer wore his khaki uniform and I wore a pink party dress that I had made in Logan. Bishop Merrill was a very quiet, dignified man and conducted an impressive ceremony—at least it seemed so to me. And so we were married.

Mother had made a cake and cocoa and served it after the ceremony.

The memory of those first few days is as vivid as if they were just yesterday. Mother had fixed up her own bedroom for us. We spent the weekend on the farm—went for a ride in the buggy, roamed about, and enjoyed our first days of marriage together.

The local newspaper, a county weekly, reported the wedding on the front page in an article titled "Popular Young Couple Married":

> Spencer W. Kimball of Thatcher and Miss Camilla Eyring of this place surprised many of their friends when they took the matrimonial oath Friday and were joined in wedlock.
>
> The bride is the daughter of Mr. and Mrs. E. C. Eyring of Pima. She is at present a member of the faculty of the Gila Academy.
>
> Mr. Kimball is a son of President and Mrs. Andrew Kimball. He is one of the drafted boys from this county and is certified for duty in the National Army. His name appears among those called for service in the next contingent from this county.
>
> At present the young couple are living in Thatcher.

**Popular Young
Couple Married**

———

Spencer W. Kimball of Thatcher
and Miss Camilla Eyring of this
place surprised their many friends
when they took the matrimonial
path Friday and were joined in wed-
lock.

The bride is the daughter of Mr.
and Mrs. E. C. Eyring of Pima.
She is at present a member of the
faculty of the Gila Academy.

Mr. Kimball is a son of President
and Mrs. Andrew Kimball. He is
one of the drafted boys from this
county and is certified for duty in
the National Army. His name ap-
pears among those called for service in the next contingent from
this county.

At present the young couple are
living at Thatcher.

*Front-page story in local weekly
newspaper*

Three weeks after the wedding Camilla's mother
wrote her daughter a loving note:

My darling, sweet little girl, Camilla,

*Twenty-three years ago today was the happiest day of
our lives, when we received our first little jewel from
heaven, and held in our arms for the first time our sweet,
blue-eyed, golden-haired baby. You have been a joy and
comfort to us ever since, and my wish is that you and
Spencer may have as long and as happy a life as your
father and I have had.*

God bless and prosper you both is the wish of your devoted mother.

Camilla and Spencer were married on Friday, and Monday morning she had to return to her work. They lived in a room at the home of Spencer's father and stepmother, since Spencer expected his military orders at any time. When the weeks passed and Spencer's leaving was postponed indefinitely, they decided to rent one side of his sister Alice's house, where they hoped to have more privacy. Alice and her husband had one long room and a long screened porch across the back of the house, and they partitioned off a small portion of the room and porch with outing flannel curtains. Camilla's mother gave the newlyweds a bed and Spencer's family gave them a few odd pieces of furniture, so they were able to scrape together enough to get along. But Alice's baby had colic and cried night and day, and with just a curtain separating the couples, there really was not much privacy. Camilla taught domestic science, and it bothered her greatly to have to make-do when she had such high ideals of how a lovely home should be.

We were married just about a month when I found that I was pregnant. This was not according to our plan. I had a contractual obligation to finish out my school year, and we had hoped to wait a while for a baby. At first I was rebellious, for the situation of being pregnant so soon embarrassed me, but there was nothing to do but stand it. My health was fine and I was never nauseated, so I managed all right.

We lived on my salary and what Spencer earned doing occasional farm labor and playing piano in a dance band.

Our living quarters were so unsatisfactory that soon after the first of the year we rented Mr. Wakefield's house across from the old Thatcher hotel. We rented it furnished for fifteen dollars a month and it was pretty ramshackle, but even so it was a mansion compared to what we had had. When it appeared that Spencer would not have to go into the service, he got a fulltime job at the Citizens Bank. With the income he bought me a wedding ring, we bought a dining table and chairs and a few other odds and ends, we paid our debts, and we began to live like other folks.

In March there was an epidemic of a rather mild form of smallpox, and before the doctors realized what it was, everyone had already been exposed, so they didn't attempt to quarantine. Spencer caught the disease and was quite sick; he had 125 pocks on his face alone. I went on teaching school, and Mother came to help take care of Spencer. That was a trying time.

Fortunately, I didn't show my pregnancy at first, so I managed to finish school in May without too much embarrassment. Then I foolishly insisted on doing extension home economics work with Brother Nash through the summer. In his old Ford we bumped over the hot, dusty roads to out-of-the-way farmhouses to help young people with home projects.

As soon as my school obligation ended, Spencer and I finally were free to go to the Salt Lake Temple to be sealed before our baby was born. We used our last penny to make the trip. By this time I was big and felt ugly, and my nerves were worn to a frazzle. I hated meeting Spencer's relatives and friends for the first time, looking like I did, and I made matters worse by being irritable. I cried almost every day the first year of our marriage. I wonder now how Spencer ever stood it. He did grow calloused and would say, "Go ahead and cry. You'll feel better when you get through."

In the temple I felt quite self-conscious because of my condition and the way I looked. Of course, I was unduly sensitive. One woman tactlessly said to me, "You surely are not going through for your own endowment, are you?" I started to cry and said, "Yes, but I have been married a long time."

But the discomfort I felt was far overshadowed by the satisfaction of knowing that Spencer and I were now husband and wife for all eternity. That feeling of security helped and sustained us over many rough spots.

When we returned home I went on working again with Brother Nash until the first of August.

In August when I went into labor, three weeks earlier than we had expected, Ben Blake went to Pima for my mother, while a neighbor stayed with me. During my agony she kept calling me "Sis," which got on my nerves till I could hardly stand it. I screamed so much that the neighbors were about to have me arrested, and my throat was sore for a week. Such agony is indescribable. The doctor who attended me was just beginning his practice as an osteopath. He didn't know much about medicine, and I have always felt that I had him to blame for the many ills that resulted from that first confinement. He did the best he knew how, but he didn't know enough. The lacerations remained raw and unhealed for years, causing me untold misery.

After all the pain, our first son, Spencer LeVan, was born August 26, 1918. His head was misshapen at first and I feared he might have suffered damage, but he soon assumed a normal look and my fears subsided. He was a precious child in whom we invested great hopes.

On the third day, when my milk came, I nearly died. My breasts were so full and my nipples so tender that they bled every time the baby nursed. And the afterpains were so bad that the nurse had to hold me in bed. The doctor had a ten-month-old child who was starving because they couldn't find any food to agree with him, so that big, bony child was brought to nurse me. The minute he came in the door he would reach out his arms and bare his teeth, and I would begin to cry.

I recovered slowly, but when LeVan was ten days old, Spencer's sister Helen was to be married, and I insisted on being carried to the wedding. I had a relapse and was in bed another two weeks.

When the baby was six weeks old I was still very miserable. We went to stay at Spencer's parents' home while they were away. One Sunday afternoon a friend came to visit and kissed me. That night she came down with the flu, and three days later I went to bed with the illness in its worst form. So then they stopped bringing the doctor's child—one gain from the flu! I was desperately ill

Camilla and her first child, Spencer LeVan

for weeks. I had one of the first cases of the terrible epidemic of 1918, and the doctors didn't know much about how to care for patients. I have marveled many times since then that I ever pulled through, for I was so weak to begin with.

LeVan grew to be a fine, husky baby. I had more milk than he could take, and I got thin while he got fat. I was never well. I did my work and went about, but felt miserable.

Even so we had fun. In July 1919, when LeVan was not quite a year old, we set out on a vacation trip to northern Arizona in two cars with some friends, the Wesley Taylors and the Bert Hoopeses.

Cars in those days had little power, and the

roads were terrible. On steep hills the passengers would get out and walk. Every little hill we came to, Wes Taylor, our driver, would say, "We'll never make it to the top of this hill. I know we'll never make it." But somehow, in spite of his pessimism each time, we did make it. We could go only about forty miles a day. The second night we were caught in the forest in the rain and found refuge at a sawmill run by the Copelands. Hospitality was never more appreciated. We finally made it to St. Johns, where we stayed with friends and celebrated the 24th of July. On our return we went through the Petrified Forest. It rained and roads were quagmire. It took a whole day of pushing and groaning to go forty miles.

When we reached the Gila River at San Carlos it was late afternoon, and we expected to reach home that night. The river was in flood, and we hired some Indians to pull us across the stream. Safely over, we found the cars would not start but would have to dry out, so we camped by the side of the river. Spencer and Bert Hoopes went behind some bushes, took off their trousers, and, holding them over their heads, waded the river and went to San Carlos to get some food. Vacations were real adventures.

When LeVan was eighteen months old I had a miscarriage—a little boy—at five months. It was a terrible shock and I was grief stricken. There followed months of misery and another miscarriage at six weeks. I continued to drag around. When I became pregnant again, the doctor put me to bed until after the fifth month.

Finally the waiting was over, and on July 31,

*Camilla and Spencer with Spencer LeVan,
6, and Olive Beth, 2*

1922, a dear baby girl came to us. We appreciated
her doubly, having had such a desperate time
trying to keep her. She had blue eyes and reddish
hair like Spencer's mother, so her Grandfather
Kimball wanted to name her Olive. We added the
name Beth for good measure.

After Olive Beth's birth, for another two years
I still did not recover. Finally I went to a doctor in
Miami, Arizona.

When he examined me he was shocked at the
condition he found and said, "My ____, woman, if
you were forty I'd say you were full of cancer." Of
course, I was scared to death and submitted to an
operation at once. He cut off a piece of tissue
about the size of the palm of one's hand and sent it
to a laboratory. It was apparently not cancerous,

only ulcerated. I was in the hospital two lonely weeks, and after two months at home, I returned for an examination, only to find that the catgut knots had not held and the dreadful ordeal was to be endured again. In another week I was put on a bed on the train to return home. This time the operation was successful and I felt like a new person. I felt really well for the first time in six years.

5

"A home of our own—it seemed like a palace!" That's how Camilla felt when Spencer was transferred to Safford, Arizona, in 1921 by his employer, the Citizens Bank, and they purchased a small white frame house. It had only three rooms plus bath and sleeping porch. She cooked on a wood stove and took a coal oil heater into the bathroom for winter bathing or washed the children in a galvanized tub by the stove. But the home was theirs, and that was the important thing. Camilla worked at home while Spencer worked long hours at extra jobs; she helped him fill out the reports he had to complete as stake clerk, and she used her homemaking skills to stretch every penny. They saved faithfully. Caught up in speculative fever of boom times, they bought bank and oil and mining stocks in sure-fire ventures. But these collapsed in the early 1920s; they lost every·cent and had to start over·

In 1922 Spencer's stepmother, "Aunt Josie," died, so he and Camilla went to live with his father in Thatcher for about a year and rented out their own home for twenty-five dollars a month.

He was very appreciative of everything and enjoyed having LeVan tag along as he worked in

77

First home owned by the Kimballs, as it looks today. Small palm tree was planted soon after purchase in 1921.

the garden, but naturally he wanted things done his way, and there were many hard situations. He would get up early. We tended to stay up later and get up later than he. During the time we were there, we entertained many of the apostles who came for conference. President and Sister Grant and their daughter were among our guests.

When Andrew Kimball married Mary Connelly, a lovely woman who was editor of the *Young Women's Journal,* Spencer and Camilla were able to return to their own home in Safford.

Over the next few years life was full for them. Spencer was a rising young businessman and community leader. He also held positions in the Church that demanded a great deal of time—stake clerk from the time of their marriage, and counselor in the stake presidency from 1924 on. Camilla was also busy with Church responsibilities. She had been a Sunday School teacher at fourteen in Mexico and had served on the stake Sunday School board in Hinckley. Three weeks after she was married she was called to serve on the stake Primary board, and later in the presidency, service that lasted twelve years. For another seven years she was a member of the Young Women's Mutual Improvement Association stake presidency. The stake extended into three states—Arizona, New Mexico, and Texas—and just to make one visit to each of the wards in a year required travel of more than two thousand miles.

Their family was growing also. On March 5, 1927, their third child was born, a boy. After the repair operations, this pregnancy had gone without complications.

> Spencer's father had died in 1924, and we named the baby Andrew for him and Eyring for my family. Andrew was strong and healthy and grew rapidly, but cried almost constantly night and day for seven months. We doctored him for colic but to no avail. Spencer and I had to take care of him in shifts to get any sleep at all. When he grew older and could indicate the source of his discomfort, we found that he had been suffering all these months with earache.

Though their responsibilities were heavy, the family found time for outings and for visits with friends and relatives. In 1926 they took LeVan and Olive Beth

Top, Camilla, LeVan, and Olive Beth at Sunset Crater in Arizona, 1925.
Bottom, Spencer, Camilla, and LeVan at Hill Cumorah, 1929.

for a trip by car through northern Arizona to Grand
Canyon and fished at Mormon Lake. "This was our
first real vacation, and we had a grand time," Camilla
recalls.

In June 1928, they bought a new Studebaker and
took the family of three children to Salt Lake City for a

visit with Andrew Kimball's widow, Mary. From there they traveled to Yellowstone, Seattle, and on to Victoria, British Columbia.

> Because this was my first trip out of the country, I wanted to buy a souvenir and bought two pelicans in a hurry. I really didn't like them much, and when I was required to pay duty on them, I felt like throwing them away, but I could not bring myself to do it.

Camilla's brother Ed and his new wife, Evelyn, lived in San Francisco. Camilla wanted to make a good impression on her new sister-in-law, so she insisted on renting a motel outside the city to bathe the family and press their clothes. The next morning they went on into the city, where Evelyn received them graciously.

In Los Angeles they visited Spencer's brother Del, who was an auditor in City Hall. When Spencer pointed out the skyscraper as Uncle Del's office, the children were duly impressed that their uncle was so rich. Because in those days tourist cabins were unfurnished, the car was piled high with bedding, pots and pans, food, luggage, and children. Del said, "Spencer, you don't have to clean out your car; if you just open the door the clutter will fall out!"

When Spencer traveled, Camilla went with him if it was at all possible. One year early in their marriage each had gone his own way for vacations. Spencer felt he needed a rest and wanted to travel; Camilla wanted to buy some furniture and knew they could not do that and travel too. After some disagreement, Spencer went alone to visit a brother and sister in California. While Spencer was away a family friend, whose wife was out of town, invited Camilla to go to a movie with him. It was all very innocent and she did not accept the invitation, but it set her thinking how important it was that married couples stay together. When Spencer returned they discussed the situation and decided that they would never do that again.

In 1930 the family went to April conference in Salt Lake City, the centennial celebration of the organization of the Church. On their way back to Arizona by train they stopped over in Los Angeles for a few days and there they saw their first talking movie. They were so excited and proud to return home and tell everyone of this new wonder and to explain that the sound and the movement of the lips were so well synchronized that you could almost believe the characters were actually talking up there on the screen.

> The first time we heard a radio broadcast, we took turns using a pair of earphones, and if we listened patiently and intently enough, once in a while we could hear a voice and distinguish an occasional word. But this was a marvel of marvels, and we talked about it for weeks. To think of sound being picked up out of the air with no wires to bring it!

Safford was just a few miles east of Thatcher and Pima, where Camilla's family lived, and she and her family made many visits back and forth. Her mother came the ten miles to Safford every week in an old buggy to see Camilla and Spencer. She brought along some fresh milk, butter, and applesauce, which often got spilled a little on the rough roads. The Eyring children loved to come along because Camilla had many more "store-bought" things than they did in

Eyring family, Pima, Arizona, 1922: Standing, Joseph, Edward, Mary, Henry, Edward Christian Eyring, Anthony, Catherine. Middle row, Caroline, Caroline Romney Eyring, Camilla with LeVan, Emma Romney Eyring holding Margaret, Isabel, Ruth. Front, Ethel, Rose, Jeneveve, LeRoy, Maurine.

Pima. Her home had a flush toilet, too, and she and Spencer traveled in the summers.

When Caroline, Camilla's sister, began teaching high school, she stayed in Safford with the Kimballs for about two years; she also helped out in Spencer's office one summer as secretary and errand girl. At their home Caroline began her courtship with Glen Miner, and Spencer and Camilla were very solicitous that she get in early.

Spencer and Camilla's family circle was completed in September 1930 with the birth of their fourth baby, whom they named Edward Lawrence—Edward for Camilla's father and Lawrence for a family friend.

It was a day of great rejoicing when we got this fine red-haired boy, for we had almost given up hope of having any more children. He was an unusually good-natured and healthy child and a constant joy.

When Eddie was just a few weeks old, Spencer's uncle, President J. Golden Kimball of the First Council of the Seventy, was to visit our stake, and Stake President Harry Payne suggested that he stay with us.

It was fall weather with cold nights. I was occupying our one good bedroom with the new baby, and we hardly dared move onto the sleeping porch with him, so for Uncle Golden we fixed as best we could the small front bedroom that we had added to the house. It had only a three-quarter-size bed. We fixed a hot water bottle for him and suggested perhaps he could lie "across corners" to make the bed long enough. We assured him that Eddie was a very good baby and never cried at night.

We were all just settled in for the night when Eddie began to cry. Spencer hastened with him into the kitchen, and for hours we did our best to keep things quiet, walking the floor with the baby.

Next morning as Uncle Golden and Spencer were driving to Thatcher to conference, he asked in his high, plaintive voice, "Spencer, why don't you take your conference visitors to the hotel where they can be comfortable?" Needless to say, that night we took him to the Olive Hotel, but at least he was anxious to eat his meals with us. He liked my cooking.

When Spencer accepted the call to serve as counselor to President Payne, that put an end to some talk about Spencer's going back to college while Camilla worked to help support the family. It did not occur to them that he should not accept the calling, even though he was only twenty-nine when it came. Camilla was the first to encourage Spencer when he had doubts about his own abilities. "Of course you can do it; you can do anything the Lord asks of you!" She provided constant support.

The Kimballs had many close friends and an active social life, with dancing and parties. Typically Spencer was at the center of the singing and joking; Camilla was at the center of the food and arrangements.

The Academy offered adult evening classes. Spencer took a music class; Camilla studied literature. She loved to read and to discuss books and ideas. Her commitment to education and to encouraging her children led her to teach LeVan to read long before he was old enough for school. He was precocious already, and she pushed him along. When he just turned six years old she took him to the principal of the Safford grade school and, by demonstrating her son's abilities, persuaded the principal to let him start in the second grade. She later had second thoughts about the social costs of having her children move too far ahead of their age group, but at the time she felt sure it was the right thing to do.

Camilla established a home, like her mother's, where Father always received the best. With her strong character there could have been friction, but she had found a man she could respect and love and support. She made the kitchen the heart of her home. There she cooked marvelous things—not fancy foods, but plain food prepared superbly: cinnamon rolls and whole wheat bread; bottled peaches, apricots, applesauce, pears, cherries, and vegetables. She made butter and cottage cheese. And she washed and ironed and sewed.

Married without a ring, she soon received a gold band, but only later an "engagement" ring. In El Paso on a stake visit she and Spencer were shopping in Kress 5-and-10-cent store when Camilla spotted a toy "diamond" ring. She said, "Oh, Spencer, I'm going to get myself an engagement ring." At dinner, a friend exclaimed, "Camilla! You've got a new diamond!" Camilla, not wanting to embarrass the woman or Spencer, accepted the comment without denial. After they returned to Safford, Spencer said, "Come on, Mama, I guess it is time we bought you an engagement ring."

In 1926 Spencer and Bishop Joseph Greenhalgh started an insurance and real estate business. The prospect of leaving the bank, with its steady salary, frightened Spencer, but Camilla had confidence in his ability to succeed in business for himself. He had grown up in the area, and through the bank and his church work he knew nearly everyone. He had intelligence and drive and a pleasing personality, Camilla reassured him.

There were lean times, particularly during the Depression. Being in business for themselves posed risks. Spencer said then, "My, wouldn't it be wonderful if we had a salary to count on." In fact, they never were worse off than they would have been with the bank job, but they could not know that. Uncertainty nagged. They left the car home and the children pulled a red wagon to the grocery store. Each month, by sacrificing all luxuries, they were able to get by and never go into debt. On the farm Camilla's parents managed to get by too, but just barely. Each family helped the other.

When cash grew scarce, business turned to barter. Many businesses had to have insurance to satisfy their mortgage conditions. Camilla, needing shoes for the children, would say, "Spencer, which shoe store owes you credit?" Rather than going where the prices were best, Camilla had to shop for groceries where the credit was. She traded milk for piano lessons. Barter meant giving up some flexibility. Camilla thought, "Oh, for the days when I could walk into a store and buy with money what I wanted!"

Being self-employed provided Spencer with flexibility for church work, whether traveling to conference or speaking or singing at funerals or visiting the sick. They plowed back into the business everything they could, both of them content to wait for the capital to grow before they would draw on it for more than necessities.

In spite of troubles around them, things seemed to go rather well for the Kimball family. The pleasant routine was jarred irreversibly, however, in September, 1933.

6

Eddie, just turning three, came home from playing at the neighbors and complained that his legs hurt. He said he had sat down hard on a block. It was apparent he had a fever, and he was vomiting. The symptoms were those common to tonsillitis, from which he often suffered. A few days later he was sitting in a chair by the front door watching the children play, and when he went to stand down, he fell to the floor. I became alarmed and took him to Dr. Butler, who examined him and said he might have a touch of rheumatism following diphtheria. The next day Dr. Butler returned and brought a colleague; they examined Eddie again. I was very much concerned and, following them to the door, asked if they thought it might be infantile paralysis—poliomyelitis. They told me emphatically that it was not. Because his leg was paralyzed, we decided to take him to Dr. Williams, a chiropractor, to see if manipulations might help. Later we were told this was the worst thing we could have done. After several treatments, the poor darling screamed the minute we came in sight of the doctor's office. Finally Dr. Williams told us that he feared polio. We were terrified. Spencer wired his brother Del in Los Angeles to make an appointment with a specialist there, and we were on our way by car. We drove through the night and arrived the next morning.

At the hospital the doctor immediately diagnosed Eddie's trouble as polio and put his legs in splints. He was furious with us because we had traveled with him across two states before the three weeks of contagion was over and had exposed numerous people. It lacked three days of the three weeks we should have been quarantined. They wired the health offices of Safford and had our family and neighbors quarantined.

On his third birthday Eddie was put in isolation for the remaining three days. He wailed as they took him away and screamed himself hoarse for us, but we could only comfort him through a crack in the door during the short visiting hours, singing and telling him stories. I could hear him hoarsely calling, "Daddy," "Mama," "I want to go home." No one who has not experienced it can know the devastating heartache I felt.

We walked back and forth on the hospital grounds powerless to do anything. We rented a room in a home across the street, where we watched and waited for the time to pass. The terror and anguish of those days remain vivid.

After Eddie was out of isolation, Spencer had to return to his business and to the family. Camilla stayed another ten long, lonely weeks in Los Angeles. She had never experienced such endless days. She thanked Spencer for a letter: "Funny how I so like to be told

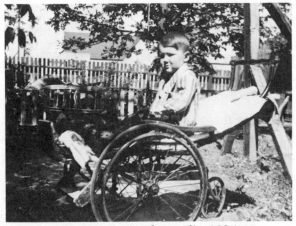

Eddie recovering from polio, 1934

that you miss me and need me. . . . Tell me about everything. You know how lonesome I will be."

Spencer urged the children to write to their
mother daily, as she was very much concerned about
them, even though her sister Mary was staying with
them and taking good care of them. Olive Beth wrote,
"Andrew is like a stubborn mule. He would not come
to eat supper with me at Mitchells' although he was
invited." Their aunt Mary was deaf and did not hear
the bickering that sometimes went on among the three
children at home. Camilla wrote about where to find
the Halloween masks and where LeVan's new shirts
were and how Olive Beth should practice her music.
"Eddie was very much distressed because I couldn't
help crying while I read your letters. After I'd quit he
kept saying, 'Are you going to cry anymore?' and
seemed relieved that I had quit."

Sometimes Eddie's condition improved, sometimes it slid back. Camilla had the elders in Los Angeles
come and administer to him again. People were kind:

Andrew mailed a squeaky elephant; Aunt Catherine sent blocks; the fruit man gave him grapes and the ice man a chunk of ice and an old lady some potato chips. But Camilla had the full responsibility. "If he just weren't such a calf for his mama." A Mr. Lytthaus had said to her, "How many times a day does he say mama? I tried to count them and it's thousands." But Camilla excused "my little leech." She entertained him with songs and stories and games day after day.

November 14, 1933

My beloved husband,

The day you receive this note will mark the sixteenth anniversary of our wedding. Our first separation on that day. I wanted to tell you again as I perhaps do too often how much I love and appreciate you. Every year increases my love and respect. This separation is bitterly hard but it has made me realize more than ever before how much I have to be thankful for. The fact that never once in the time of our acquaintance have I found cause to doubt or mistrust is I consider one of the foundation stones upon which real happiness and contentment in marriage are built. The attraction of sex and other things, of course, combine to make the perfect union, but without confidence there can be nothing lasting.

I feel that our trouble has drawn us even closer together in spirit though temporarily we are separated.

My constant prayer is that God will preserve the unity of our family and that we may soon all be together again. The joy of that day will be unmeasurable.

How I long for you and the strength received from your beautiful character. There is no other so fine and so true.

Your devoted wife,
Camilla

Tuesday morning

My darling wife,

*. . . Sixteen years is a long time for a girl to put up
with one man, and especially such a poor excuse as I am,
so I honor you on this anniversary. It has been an
extremely happy sixteen years. We have had our ups and
downs, our disappointments and our surprises, our joys
and our sorrows, and it has been a wonderful period. I
want you to know that I love and appreciate you. You are
the finest wife in the world and I am not unmindful of it
even though I do seem thoughtless at times. . . .*

Affectionately,
Spencer

LeVan's letters were full of sports and church activities, reading and public speaking activities; at fifteen
he earned his football letter. Olive Beth, eleven, reported she was the only student in the seventh grade to
get a perfect score in arithmetic. "I played marbles
with Andrew last night. He beat me all to pieces."
Andrew and Olive Beth built a dog house. Andrew,
six, wrote, "I have 38 marbles."

Finally, in December Camilla brought Eddie home,
having learned to splint his legs and massage and heat
and exercise them. For the next eight years summers
involved trips to Los Angeles for Eddie's checkups and
operations on his legs and feet. No one can count
either the hours or the concern she expended on this
beloved child.

One of their friends asked, "Why did this have to
happen to you? You've always lived such a good life."
But Camilla did not see illness as God's punishment,
nor necessarily as a specific test of faith or strength.
Perhaps those were the true explanations, but so far as

she could see the Lord left a great many things to operation of natural causes—a matter of infection and too little resistance, with the Lord letting us make of experience what we can.

When Eddie started school in the fall of 1936 and walked in front of the playground slide, a boy coming down the slide struck Eddie's leg just above the ankle and broke it. Camilla grieved at what seemed to her just too much. But despite her special sympathy, she tried not to treat him in any special way. She and Spencer expected him to do chores just as the others did, and succeeded in helping him feel capable, not handicapped.

Spencer was away on church assignments a great deal, so much of the child rearing fell to Camilla, but she supported him in his positions unwaveringly. She also added Relief Society stake board to her church experience. There was always prayer in the Kimball home; they knelt at the family table night and morning, and all took their turns in offering the prayer. They held family home evenings whenever the children could catch Spencer with an evening free. Each person performed, they played games, and Camilla always provided refreshments.

Camilla worked hard in the home, bending over the washtubs, scrubbing clothes on a washboard, sweat dripping off her face. With a big hat to protect her fair skin, she planted and watered and weeded the garden. She strained the milk and skimmed the cream. Sometimes she treated herself to the thickest cream from a small crock in the refrigerator, dipping it out with a bread crust. She was a fine cook, whose meals of leftovers tasted as good the second or third time. A turkey dinner became successively casserole and chow mein

Spencer and Camilla with Spencer LeVan,
16; Olive Beth, 12; Andrew, 8; Edward, 4,
in Safford, Arizona, 1935

or stew. She boiled the bones and skin for broth, then boiled them again for soup stock. Her father, not so generous with her mother's cooking, said, "Nothing Camilla cooks ever hurts me."

She followed the current dietary notions and kept the children from putting sugar on their cereal. Spencer might do it, and they could choose for themselves when they grew up, but current lore had it that sugar and milk together in the stomach caused fermentation.

The family traveled together often. To pay for their trips, they worked at saving in little ways. The children learned not to ask for soda pop or candy bars, and they walked to school and to church instead of using the car. When they traveled, they carried their own food instead of patronizing restaurants. To pass the time in travel, they would memorize scriptures or the Articles of Faith in English or Spanish, and they memorized hymns, each taking a turn to sing a favorite one. Or they would guess the distance to a bend in the road or a distant hill, or play word games.

On holidays and every Sunday afternoon after church the whole family drove to the Eyring grandparents' home in Pima, even the teenagers, who occasionally had to be coaxed. Spencer and the boys sometimes pulled on overalls and helped their grandfather with the chores. Grandfather had a quiet, relaxed way about him, and it was fun to visit and just dawdle along. Then there were Aunt Emma's children to play with and ride horses with. Grandfather was always willing to put the saddle on Betty the Shetland or on his big pinto. Sometimes they played in the wash down a steep incline behind the house. Always Grandmother had good fruit and bread and milk, and sometimes cookies or an occasional cream pie. There was even a certain adventure in using the outhouse, with its Sears catalog on a nail.

In 1935 Camilla and Spencer went to Mexico City, and they brought back some souvenirs: serapes, straw hats, and a guitar. Andrew and Eddie were taught some Mexican songs to sing, and Andrew learned how to strum the guitar. Camilla carted them all over the Gila Valley to perform for church groups, clubs, and parties.

When Camilla's sister Catherine turned eighteen and graduated from high school, Camilla and Spencer invited her to go with them on a trip by train to Chicago—a great adventure, for she had never been out of the state of Arizona since the family moved there in 1912. They rode in the chair car all the way and feasted on box lunches Camilla had prepared.

When the train stopped in New Orleans en route to Chicago, Spencer left for a short time and returned carrying two large brown paper bags filled to overflowing with bananas. He said, "Now you have all the bananas you can eat." Nothing could have pleased Camilla and Catherine more, because in all their lives they had never had many bananas. The three managed to eat every banana before they reached Chicago.

Camilla loved to play bridge. She belonged to a bridge club that met to play once or twice a week. She played well and often won the token prizes offered at the parties. She faithfully read the newspaper columns on bridge. In 1936 Elder Melvin J. Ballard came to the stake to hold conference and preached a sermon calling on the bridge players to give up their game. This hit hard and distressed Camilla. She could see no harm in bridge, but she had to admit that she suffered from an addiction. It consumed a great deal of her time that might have been put to better use. Considering the source of the advice, she and her friends resolved to make the sacrifice and conform.

In 1936 Spencer was called to be president of the Mount Graham Stake when it was created by division of the St. Joseph Stake, in which he had served as stake clerk or counselor, or both, since their marriage. This broadened his responsibilities and, likewise, Camilla's. People now looked to her for example even more than before. She disliked the role, but she filled it well.

In 1931 Spencer had served as president of the

Safford Rotary Club. In that role he promoted a number of service activities, particularly the Boy Scout movement and free lunches for poor children. His friends urged him to run for the position of district governor; no Mormon in Arizona had held that position. Before the district convention in 1935 he campaigned hard, only to learn on arriving at the convention that the principal opponent's campaign manager had just died of a heart attack. Rather than promote a heated contest under the circumstances, Spencer, with the consent of the men who had worked for his election, stood and withdrew his candidacy and nominated his opponent. The generous gesture stunned the crowd, who afterward swarmed around to express their admiration. Spencer noted, "I became somewhat of a hero all at once without meriting it." But the next year, when he decided to run again, he had no opposition.

He and Camilla traveled throughout the state of Arizona that year, nearly wearing out a car visiting each of the twenty-three clubs at least once. Spencer felt comfortable out front in public, but Camilla disliked the limelight. However, she greatly appreciated small attentions—flowers, a token gift acknowledging her presence, a word of welcome—and she noted them all in a journal she kept. She also noted the compliments: "You seem too young to have an eighteen-year-old son!" And she wrote, as the year neared its close:

It was a very pleasant experience but I really do not crave publicity. I am satisfied to go quietly my own way. I do feel that much worthwhile development has come from the contacts through Rotary this year and I have appreciated it as an

opportunity to grow. I have a real ambition to
learn to be quietly at ease under any circumstances and in any company, to take my place in a
dignified yet simple manner. I dislike a pompous
air and I do seek to be genuinely cordial.... I
never expect to come as near the center of the
stage again.

During the year Spencer organized four new clubs
in the district, a record number. In appreciation the
district unexpectedly voted to pay his travel expenses
to the international convention in Nice, France. He
and Camilla jumped at the chance to go to Europe.
They dipped into their savings and borrowed on their
insurance policy for Camilla's expenses. This was the
opportunity of a lifetime. They had traveled across the
United States, but never dreamed they could go to
Europe. Almost no one they knew had been to Europe,
except on a mission.

LeVan was serving his mission in Montreal and
they arranged to sail from there so they could visit him.
They spent several days sightseeing before their ship
left. At the wax museum they nudged one another and
laughed at the guard who had fallen asleep at his post,
reading a newspaper, then laughed at themselves as
they realized he was wax, too.

On the ocean aboard the *Duchess of Athol*, they saw
whales and icebergs, danced, and ate, even when the
seas became rough. In France they stayed up all night
sightseeing in Paris before catching a train for Nice in
the morning, giddy from sleeplessness. The convention itself in Nice proved an exciting time, with cama-
raderie, fireworks, dancing, pageantry. The convention over, they undertook to see everything they could

Left, aboard the Duchess of Athol, *en route to Rotary convention in Nice, France. Right, at Mount Vesuvius, 1937.*

in south-central Europe—Italy, Switzerland, Hungary, Austria, Germany, the Netherlands, France, and England. They often traveled through the night to save hotel costs and to leave days for sightseeing. They wanted to make the trip memorable.

Italy interested them the most. Here were art treasures, Roman ruins, Vesuvius, the Vatican. Christian history came alive for them—the catacombs, the arena where early saints had been put to fight the lions, the Vatican and St. Peter's Cathedral as the seat of Roman Catholicism. They had also both read *The Last Days of Pompeii* and walked fascinated through the excavated streets of that city; they climbed Vesuvius and brought home a blob of lava that their guide pulled out of a fissure with an iron bar and formed around an Italian coin before it hardened.

Venice proved the most romantic place on the trip. The city, built on islands, was criss-crossed with waterways. They had a grand moonlit gondola ride, enjoying being together. But they had been gone from their children a month and had received no letters, and Camilla felt pangs of homesickness.

In Budapest they asked the hotelier to suggest an entertainment and he recommended the show at the Arizona Club. The name attracted them and they went to the nightclub. To justify seeing the show they had to buy a drink so they selected the cheapest item on the drink list and were served a thimbleful of liquor. They enjoyed the show, on a circular stage behind a water screen, but the liquor still sat there as they left; Spencer did not touch his, while Camilla only tasted hers, curious to see what liquor tasted like.

In Brussels Camilla was told to be sure to see Mannike Pis and she asked the guide to be sure they did not miss it. As they traveled about the city she several times asked for reassurance that they were not going to miss that statue and fountain and the guide said yes, yes, they would come to it. Finally he brought them to an intersection where they could see the memorial to a little boy who had been lost and then found. Camilla blushed to see that it was a statue of the boy as he had been found, naked and forever urinating into a pool. To tease Camilla, Spencer insisted that they buy a little replica of the statue.

They bought wooden shoes in Holland, climbed the Eiffel Tower, took a riverboat down the Rhine, entered the ice caves in a Swiss glacier. They traveled hard, seeing every museum, castle, and cathedral in their path, thinking this their one chance to make places and things they had only read about come to life.

But finally, in London near the end of the ten-week whirlwind tour, Camilla confided to her journal, "I am so downright homesick tonight I just had to cry a bit. I wish I could fly home. I have seen so much I have reached the saturation point. Nothing seems interesting anymore. Our expenses are so high I am quite in the dumps. . . . I shall be most happy to go home to my own little niche and let the rest of the world go by."

When they finally boarded the *Berengaria* Camilla went to bed exhausted and slept and slept.

7

In 1940 the Kimball family moved into a new home that they had painstakingly planned and watched step by step in the building. For years they had taken pictures, gathering ideas, of Southwestern architecture in Tucson, Phoenix, Albuquerque, El Paso, and in between. The six-room home in pueblo style was not elaborate nor expensive, but for them it was "a mansion and built of love and dreams." They planned it as a unit. The furniture was all new, much of it Monterey style purchased after long consideration at Barker Brothers in Los Angeles. Indian pictures hung on the walls. The bedspreads carried Indian design, and Camilla embroidered curtains to match. They planned and planted a garden and an orchard, had a barn with cows, chickens, and a pig—in fact, they felt they had established an estate where they could end their days.

Camilla took great pride in the new home and in the yard they planted. Along the north side of the lot was a row of oleanders, which grew as tall as the house. On either side of the long driveway they planted a cactus garden. The family went by car out into the hills to gather the cactus plants. One was a rare night-blooming cereus, and when it bloomed for one night, the air of the whole neighborhood was scented. And

Camilla and Spencer, about 1938

there were sweet peas, nasturtiums, zinnias, holly-
hocks, irises, roses, and climbing vines.

From the time they were very small the children
helped around the house and in the yard. The daughter helped her mother with cleaning and cooking,
canning, sewing, baby tending, and so on. The sons all
helped with mowing the lawn, irrigating the yard (a
tedious chore during the hot, dry summers), chopping
weeds, picking pecans, mending fences, scything hay
or weeds, feeding and milking the cows, and shoveling
the corrals. Sometimes they rebelled at the work, but
their parents were determined that it was good for
them.

When the children finished their chores, their parents found more things to keep them busy. Andrew at
fourteen had spare time during the summer, so
Spencer talked a friend who managed the local Sears
Roebuck store into offering the youth some work.

New pueblo-style house built in 1940, Safford, Arizona

Andrew was legally too young to work for the store, so the manager paid him out of his own pocket.

Kimball-Greenhalgh, the family business, hired the boys to clean up vacant lots so they would sell more easily, or fix up properties left in chaos by renters, so they could be rented again. Olive Beth learned to type and to file letters accurately in her father's business, and she saw firsthand how honorable and kind he was in all his dealings. She also made enough money to see her through school.

LeVan and his father built a corral and a small barn. Neither structure cost them a cent. LeVan pulled nails out of scrap lumber from an old barn and fence posts on some property his father had bought, and he had the task of straightening the nails. Spencer and Camilla were very economical; between the fruit trees they planted alfalfa that was scythed by hand; every day they separated and sold to the creamery the cream from the milk of their cows. Camilla made and remade clothes, preserved fruit and vegetables and jams, and always shopped the sales. Thrift was more than a conscious virtue, it was a character trait.

The children were taught to be thrifty and to handle money, too. They were paid for doing chores around the house—ten cents for catching a mouse, twenty-five cents for hoeing the garden, fifty cents for doing the weekly irrigating, seventy-five cents a week for milking the cows, and so on. What each child did not need for gifts or movies or personal pleasures, their parents would encourage them to put into the family business. It was a lot of bother and did not amount to very much, but it taught them to work and save. Over the years with compound interest it helped with missions and school, and they also learned how to figure and pay their tithing on their earnings.

Sometimes LeVan would forget to milk the family cows, and he would feel sheepish when his father, without comment, went out late after his work and church meetings to do the work. That helped his memory better than a switching or scolding would have done. Andrew would pretend he was asleep when the family returned home from a picnic and the cows were bellowing to be milked. While Camilla put him to bed, Spencer milked the cows.

Birthdays were very special occasions, with a tiered cake and friends over to a big birthday party. At Christmas Santa brought most of the things the children had asked for—and even some things they had forgotten about. The parents were adroit at making the children think they did not really want those things they couldn't or shouldn't have. Santa's handwriting looked very much like Camilla's, and last-minute gifts were likely to appear under the tree in brown paper sacks. Spencer always read off the names on gifts

Camilla with Olive Beth, Andrew, and
Edward, Long Beach, California, 1939

under the tree. One year he purposely ignored the
gifts placed there by Olive Beth's boyfriend. "Well, I
guess that's all," he said, pretending not to see the
remaining gifts. An embarrassed Olive Beth had to
point them out.

Spencer teased; Camilla did not, although she was
good natured about the teasing she received from
Spencer and the children, including the retelling of
the time a farmer named his cow after her and of the
old man who, on meeting her, said, "Oh yes, you are
one of the plain-faced Eyring girls." Eddie once gave

his mother such a vigorous hug that he cracked her ribs.

The children occasionally needed disciplining. When Olive Beth was very small, her father came home one day to find her wearing two of his hats—on her feet! He spanked her, for the only time in her life. Another time when he asked Olive Beth to help her mother with the dishes, she answered, "Just a minute," and turned back to reading her book. Her father snatched the book, flung it across the room, and scolded her. Afterward Camilla consoled her, saying that that action was just his letting off steam from a bad day at the office.

But generally Spencer and Camilla were in complete accord. Though they disagreed at times, they never argued in front of the children.

Camilla's reaction to the misbehavior of her children could be unnerving. Her usual discipline consisted of a glare and a scolding, but when LeVan took the scissors to Olive Beth's carefully nurtured, long blonde hair and snipped off the curls, Camilla reacted with a torrent of tears. There was no whipping for him, but tears were worse. Then when he was about ten years of age, LeVan became a consignment salesman for *Literary Digest*. He grew to hate the task, and one week in frustration he hid his unsold copies of the magazine behind the garage and told his mother he had sold them. A week later Camilla stumbled across them. As when he cut off Olive Beth's curls, she burst into tears. When Spencer came home, LeVan was ordered to cut a willow switch from a tree, but again, all the good that punishment could do was already done by Camilla's tears.

During these years Camilla was active in the Saf-

ford Federated Women's Club. The club maintained
the public library, and she spent several years as the
volunteer librarian. Just as she had once read books
under the covers as a child, so now she continued to
keep up with the best sellers and classics. She had a
great ambition to be well read, and she was eager to
share her literary discoveries with others. She gave
book reviews to gatherings in Safford, including some
over the radio, and she encouraged her children to
read good literature. In the summer she and the children would sometimes make a list of books to be read,
and she would mark them off as they were completed.

Olive Beth went through a period of hating to
read. Then one day she found that if she were reading,
her mother would let her out of doing the dishes, so
every night after supper she would pick up a book and
become engrossed for a few minutes, until the dishes
were done. In the process she found that she truly
became interested in books.

Under the law at the time, Camilla's marriage to
Spencer had given her American citizenship. Not long
before that, women in the United States had been
made eligible to vote. Camilla had some interest in
politics and served as a poll worker during elections as
a civic service.

Camilla served as first president of the Safford
PTA, as president of the Safford Women's Club, and
as president of the Southeastern Arizona Federation
of Women's Clubs. The latter experience gave her
contact with many women outside her own community
and led to her being recommended as secretary of the
state federation. She would have been eager to accept
the position and broaden her sphere, but that was the
year the Kimballs left Arizona and moved to Utah.

As the children moved into their teens, their problems changed and Camilla had to adjust. She had the patience and ability to listen to their questioning arguments. They each in turn argued radical, doubting, or antiestablishment positions with her. She would discuss at whatever length they wished to pursue the subject, reasonably, without heat. She never "won" an argument, yet somehow her values, opinions, and points of view generally became theirs. The arguments served as a means of testing and learning. She sometimes felt despair and disappointment at the expressed attitudes and opinions, but by and large she really prevailed. These discussions took place in the kitchen, the most intimate room in the home, as Camilla went about her work.

As the children started dating they had rules and regulations to follow. Olive Beth was told that if a party let out at ten, she was to be home by ten thirty; if it let out at twelve, she was to be home by twelve thirty. She managed to keep the curfew, though it was awkward on occasion. Camilla always stayed awake, reading, no matter how late, until the children were all home.

When Andrew returned home from a date with his first serious girl friend at age sixteen, his mother expressed concern the next day when she discovered lipstick on his handkerchief; she warned him of the need to be on guard.

Friends set their standards by those of the Kimballs. If the Kimball children were going to a party or movie, their friends could go; if not, then the friends could not go either. This fact added to their feeling of responsibility in regard to their standards. But they were never coerced into accepting their parents' standards; they were encouraged to work things out for themselves. Once, after Sunday dinner, the boys began to play table tennis and a prospective daughter-in-law asked Spencer how it was that they played on Sunday. He replied, "I don't do it, but they must decide for themselves."

Camilla had a philosophy about religious problems that helped her children. She said that when things troubled her, she put them on the shelf; later when she looked at them again, some were answered, some seemed no longer important, and some needed to go back on the shelf for another time. She bore her testimony in meetings less often than she would have liked, because she tended to weep and her children became embarrassed.

Olive Beth and her mother had a special mother-daughter relationship. Recalling her own trial of being at school with no proper clothes, Camilla made sure her daughter felt comfortable about her clothing. Olive Beth always had at least one outfit with matching shoes, purse, hat, and dress, and she was allowed to pick out her own dress patterns. Camilla was an excellent seamstress and made much of the family's clothing. The children never felt rich, but they never felt uncomfortable because they did not have the right things to wear.

Culture was also encouraged in their home. Each of the children had music lessons, though they did not all continue their interest in music into adulthood. LeVan had many piano lessons, but when he learned his parents hoped he might be a concert pianist, he rebelled and quit completely. Olive Beth learned to play the piano and violin well and also participated in school singing groups and later the Tabernacle Choir. Andrew and Edward followed suit with music lessons

of various kinds. Camilla had to police the practicing.
She regretted not having learned to play the organ
well in Mexico, and determined that her children
should do better. She had practiced with a novel
propped on the organ and smiled when she found
some of her children doing the same thing.

All of the children excelled in their school studies
and activities. When Andrew graduated from junior
high school, Spencer wrote, "Last night we were
mighty proud of Andrew. About fifteen others were
cited for being outstanding in one field or another—
art, music, athletics—but Andrew topped them all.
Was I proud?"

Olive Beth felt she had to do well in school because
her parents expected her to, and she couldn't let them
down. LeVan and Edward were also honor graduates.

While academics received the warmest response
from Spencer and Camilla, they always supported any
activity—musical, forensic, athletic. When Andrew
was playing basketball his mother would often come to
the games, but she found it distressing. She would
become extremely emotional and would cheer loudly
for her boy to "come through for Mother."

Threads of love were woven through the fabric of
Camilla. She had great pride in and concern for each
child; she motivated by encouragement, not by
threats. All of the sons filled missions for the Church.
LeVan was called to the Eastern Canadian Mission
when he was only seventeen; he had already completed two years of college, which was the alternate
requirement at that time to being twenty years of age.
Andrew filled a mission after World War II in New
England, and Edward went at eighteen to the Netherlands.

All of the children, as they left the family home for missions, college, and marriage, took with them the unwavering support of their parents. There was never a moment of doubting their father's and mother's complete love for them.

8

In November 1942 Camilla and Spencer observed their silver wedding anniversary. Twenty-five years had passed since they had spoken their vows at the Eyring home in Pima. To celebrate, they decided to have an open house. Though World War II was on and gas had been rationed, friends and relatives came from Phoenix, Tucson, and many other communities around, all wishing to share in the occasion. They sent 600 invitations for staggered times, beginning at two o'clock in the afternoon, but almost no one would go home, and by the evening's end their small house bulged with people happily suffering the crowding to stay and visit. They had made their niche secure, surrounded by friends and family.

On July 8, 1943, only a few months after our celebration, when all seemed comfortable in our little world, a veritable bomb struck our household. Spencer and the children came home at midday for dinner, our big meal of the day. Dinner was all ready as Spencer came in the door. The telephone rang and Eddie answered; the operator said, "Salt Lake calling for Spencer Kimball." Spencer took the phone and I could tell from the

113

Family at time of Spencer's call to apostleship in 1943: Olive Beth, LeVan's wife Kathryn, Camilla, LeVan, first grandchild Barbara, Spencer, Andrew, Edward

look on his face and his exclamations that something most unusual and unexpected was happening.

"Surely you can't mean me, President Clark! . . . It seems impossible. . . . Can I come to Salt Lake and talk to you?" When he finished he was pale and trembling and lay down on the floor—as he did most every day to rest a few minutes—and started to cry, exclaiming, "I could never do that!"

Then he told me that President J. Reuben Clark said they wished to call him to be one of the Quorum of the Twelve Apostles. At a recent conference, five Assistants to the Twelve Apostles had been sustained. It had been my idea that the next member of the Quorum would be selected from this group, so I said, "Are you sure it wasn't to be one of the Assistants?" Spencer assured me they had said one of the Twelve. The consternation that we both felt would be hard to describe. We were to tell no one, so we could only worry and cry together. Spencer kept saying, "I am not good enough, not big enough for such a job." I did my best to reassure him. All his life he had been faithfully dedicated to the Church and had been outstanding in his service. I knew he could do it if the Lord had called him. I was willing to give my support.

I had been ill for a month or so, hemorrhaging so badly the doctor had been unable to stop it. This new anxiety didn't help my condition. We had been planning to go on the train to El Paso to hold ward conference and then on up to Boulder, Colorado, to visit LeVan and his wife, Kathryn, where he was studying Japanese at the Navy language school. We decided we would proceed with the plan, and then I would stay in Boulder while Spencer went to Salt Lake City and back.

While we were in El Paso, the bishopric took us to dinner at the hotel, and as we ate, Brother Pauly kept saying, "Brother Kimball, who do you think will be the new apostle? Can you make a guess?" Spencer assured him, "I can't say." Little did they realize they were talking to the new member. It was uncommon to call a General Authority from outside Utah, though President Clark had been one such person. It was hard not to give the news away, for we were both so depressed that anyone should have guessed that something was up.

We couldn't even tell LeVan and Kathryn, and they wondered what was the matter with us. Spencer had been praying fervently for six days and I had been praying for him. While we were in Boulder he went alone into the hills and came back hours later with the assurance he had sought from the Lord. I was deeply grateful for that. It was a great relief when Spencer had his interview with the First Presidency in Salt Lake City and they decided to publish the news of his call immediately. It created a special stir to have a man from Arizona appointed.

Many adjustments had to be made, and there would be more and more as time went on. Olive Beth was working in San Francisco, and just Andrew and Eddie were at home with us. It was a real blow to my father and mother, who had always counted on our being near them in their declining years. We wondered if we would have a private life of our own.

Spencer began the difficult process of selling the business and our home. I was still very ill, and we finally decided to go to Salt Lake City in August so I could enter the hospital for medical care and so we could start the boys in school the first of September.

It was hard to leave. Arizona had been our only home together. The boys resented being uprooted. I hated leaving our dream house and my parents. But we went because we had been called.

This was war time. Housing in Salt Lake City was impossible to find. We registered at the Temple Square Hotel and then I went to the hospital, where they gave me twenty-four hours of radium treatment. This stopped the bleeding, but it also made me weak and nervous for many weeks.

We finally found a house available for rent in November. The problem was where to live until then. Housing was so scarce that we couldn't even rent a motel by the month. Finally Spencer's cousin Vi Woolley came to our rescue and very generously offered to let us live with her. She was unmarried and was living alone in the old family home with plenty of room, but it meant taking in a whole new family.

Andrew had been very rebellious about having to leave Safford, where all his friends and school ties were. It was to be his last year in high school. He was playing in football and basketball, was in line for scholastic honors, and had friends who meant more than family. Eddie hated the move also, but he was four years younger and was not so deeply affected.

Olive Beth came from San Francisco to be with us. Spencer went back to Safford to take care of his business. The boys started school, Andrew at East High and Eddie at Roosevelt Junior High. It meant a long bus ride for each of them. They were just getting somewhat adjusted when a polio epidemic broke out and all schools, churches, movies were closed—all public gatherings stopped. Here were these two active, unhappy boys penned up in a strange place. I was still weak and in my nervous condition I felt as if I were caged with two wild lions.

Camilla wrote to Spencer about the troubles with the boys and about her feelings:

> *Dearest Dad, ...*
> *It seems harder and harder for me to be reconciled to this move. You seemed to realize it from the start so much better than I. With me it is getting worse and worse the more I am brought to face it. I am so desperately homesick I am really ill from it. I can't seem to see any recompense in all the sacrifice ahead of us. . . . I am afraid I forgot to thank you for the chocolates, darling. I do appreciate them and thanks a million. I do love you so much. Troubles don't seem anything when you are with us but loom to mountains when you are away.*

Spencer wrote a long letter to the children, appealing for help:

> *I am not complaining, but you must know that this is not easy for Mother and me. If you could have walked with us down the mental trails of anguish the past two months you would know what I mean. One sister told me last Sunday: 'I didn't realize that there could be anything*

*in such a call but one great joy.' I have lost 18 pounds in
these two sleepless months. Your mother and I have gone
and are going through an unparallelled experience of
our lives. I am writing this letter at 4:45 A.M. to you.*

*Don't misunderstand me. I am not minimizing the
glory of this great call. On the contrary it is so great and
glorious that I am finding it so difficult to rise to
it.... This is such a great responsibility for such a little
man. You can help me so much. I promise you I will do
my best to qualify and bring you honor....*

We thought that maybe if Andrew could get
some kind of job, he might be more content. All
the time he kept insisting he was going back to
Safford. I had trouble coping and could not hold
him. Finally I called Spencer on the phone and
told him the situation. We decided that we had
better let Andrew go back to Arizona at least for a
short visit. In the meantime I persuaded him to
make one last try for a job. The Fetzers gave him
work pouring glue in their cabinet factory, and
that saved the day. School opened again in a short
time, and both boys soon made a satisfactory
adjustment and found fine friends.

About this time Spencer wrote to Olive Beth:

*You've got the sweetest mother in the world, so I hope
you will save her all you can so you will have one a long
time. You can never know how much I have missed my
mother—what an unquenchable yearning I have felt so
often, when I was younger especially, for a mother who
could understand and love and appreciate and spoil me.
Don't let the sun ever go down without having thanked*

*the Lord for such a dear mother, and let her know often,
too, for parents sometimes get hungry for expressed
affection. . . .*

At the October conference Spencer was sustained to his new calling, and then I went with him
back to Safford to make the final move. First we
celebrated Mother and Father's fiftieth wedding
anniversary and had a fine celebration with all the
children coming home for the occasion. In the
meantime we were packing, selling, and giving
away our possessions, the accumulation of twenty-
six years of married life. The house and most of
the furniture were sold to Emil Crockett, who with
others also bought the business. Many things we
gave to Mother. We packed ninety-four boxes,
trunks, and bundles to be shipped to Salt Lake
City, among them six sets of springs and mat-
tresses which we had bought new for our new
home. Many of the boxes were filled with old
letter files that Spencer's father had accumulated
and that Spencer had never had time to sort fully.
We really didn't have time to sort out many useless
things, so we just moved them.

There was much sorrow in leaving life-long
friends, my parents, who needed us so much, our
many civic and church activities, all the old famil-
iar things. We had been considered quite important members of the small community, and now
we were expected to take our place in a large
community, among important people. We felt
very inadequate.

The Arizona stakes gave us an impressive tes-
timonial. They gave Spencer a beautiful watch,

and both of us suitcases. Many kind things were said, many goodbye parties given. We may have moved away, but we never stopped being small-town folks.

In November of 1943 we moved into the lovely Doxey home. We were very fortunate to have had this experience. It was in a lovely neighborhood, and the home was beautifully furnished with all the conveniences. It gave us a feeling of adequacy that we could not have had in poorer surroundings.

On the first Thursday of each month the wives of the General Authorities meet for a luncheon and program at the Lion House. My first experience there still leaves me trembling. All my life I had thought of these women as being a superior group, on a high pedestal, whom I looked up to from afar. Suddenly I was in the midst of them and supposed to be one of them. If I were to face a firing squad, I couldn't be more terrified than I was to face that group of women that day. Most of them were older than I and had been reared in the city, while I was an inexperienced, unsophisticated, self-conscious country child. Thank goodness that after a few years I felt quite at home with them!

Camilla was called to the stake Relief Society board as the spiritual living leader soon after she moved to Salt Lake City, which also helped her feel more at home.

In November 1943, shortly after the Kimballs moved to Salt Lake City, Grant Mack came home from his mission. He had been courting Olive Beth before he left, but she had not committed herself. Now he proposed a quick marriage, since he would be going into the Navy soon. He and Olive Beth went to her parents' bedroom at one o'clock in the morning and broke the news. Spencer had been involved in a distressing excommunication action in the Twelve the day before. As they lay sleepless "here came another shock. How could we give our only daughter in marriage?"

On December 8 Grant and Olive Beth were married in the Salt Lake Temple, and her parents held open house for them that evening at home. The family had been in Salt Lake City only a few weeks. They knew very few people, so the guest list was quite small. Even so, the guests strained the facilities of the home. As a highlight of the evening Jessie Evans Smith, wife of Joseph Fielding Smith, sang a solo. The couple had a short honeymoon before Grant went into the Navy. Olive Beth continued working in Salt Lake City until he completed his basic training. Then she joined him in San Diego until he was sent to Hawaii. She came home to live with her family until he was released when the war was over.

LeVan and Andrew also served in the Navy, LeVan as a Japanese translator and Andrew as an electronics technician. Eddie was still in high school.

9

Among the choicest opportunities that came to Camilla and Spencer by reason of his position were the many visits to the stakes and missions of the Church. Ordinarily the General Authorities traveled each week to stake conferences without their wives, but on occasion and often when they went on extended mission tours their wives accompanied them. Meeting the missionaries and the Saints was thrilling—and seeing the various countries added a bonus. They never ceased to marvel at the devotion of the Saints and at the loving attention accorded to the visitors as servants of the Lord. But Camilla was reminded that her role was primarily to support her husband when she overheard a woman say, "I don't mind the men, but why do they have to bring their wives?"

During one of their supervisory visits, to the Eastern States Mission in 1945, word came from Salt Lake City that President Heber J. Grant had died, and Spencer was directed to come home at once. The mission tour was almost completed, but he left the next day for Salt Lake City. Camilla was eager for Eddie to have the tour of Washington, D.C., they had planned, so she and Eddie remained a few days to visit the nation's capital before returning home also.

A week after President Grant's death the Council of the Twelve named George Albert Smith to preside as the eighth president of the Church. Camilla had come to know him as a gentle, kindly man who went out of his way to speak to her.

As one of his early acts, President Smith assigned Spencer to work with the Indians, opening up a new area of responsibility and experience for Camilla, too.

That year they toured the Spanish-American Mission with President and Sister Lorin Jones. Starting in Fresno, California, they met with missionaries and Spanish-speaking Saints. They traveled through California to Tijuana, across California, Arizona, New Mexico, and to the southern tip of Texas. They visited the Pueblo Indians in New Mexico. Sister Jones had worked among them doing social work. She and Brother Jones had been in their homes, teaching them to cook and can food and helping with their agricultural problems. They had a thorough schooling in Indian lore and Indian culture. Camilla took home pottery samples of the various tribes and used them many times in giving talks about the Indians, seeking to build up understanding and support for the Indian work. She saw dirt and poverty, but also beauty.

> Coming into the pueblo of Taos just about sunset and seeing the village silhouetted against the evening sky was impressive. There were dozens of men in their bright-colored blankets standing on different levels of the pueblo getting the warmth from the western walls. One figure, draped in a white blanket, stood on the very top of the many-storied apartment pueblo. I wondered at first if it were a statue, he stood still for so long silhouetted against the evening sky.

Mission tours were not vacations, especially with the pace Spencer set. In 1946 Elder Matthew Cowley, suffering from heart trouble, was sent with Spencer to visit Hawaii, partly for a rest. Camilla exclaimed, "Imagine sending someone with Spencer Kimball for a rest!"

One advantage of living in Salt Lake City was the ready access to educational opportunities. Almost continuously from the time she moved to Utah Camilla took classes at the University of Utah—English, philosophy, typing, botany, history, public speaking, Bible studies, and especially literature. Other times she enrolled at the Institute of Religion. At one point she concluded that she had amassed nearly enough credits to obtain a college degree, but she discovered to her disappointment that the university considered outdated the college credits she had earned as a young woman.

Her own great interest in education helped influence her family to seek a good education at any cost. Among them the fifteen of her father's children who lived to maturity earned twenty-four college degrees, not counting Henry's additional fifteen honorary degrees. Eleven of the children had substantial experience as teachers. They tended to marry people with similar aspirations: their spouses had twenty college degrees (plus Spencer's several honorary ones), and seven of them were teachers.

Camilla's own four children earned ten college degrees among them, and three became teachers. There was always a dictionary by the kitchen table, ready for consultation when a question arose about words.

> I have always had an inquiring mind. I am not satisfied just to accept things. I like to follow through and study things out. I learned early to put aside those gospel questions that I could not answer. I had a shelf of things I did not understand, but as I have grown older and studied and prayed and thought about each problem, one by one I have been able to understand them better.
>
> A woman, to be well rounded in her personality, needs many experiences in and out of the home. She needs to be concerned with church, school, and community. If she buries herself inside four walls, she does not reach her potential. She needs to keep growing, to keep aware of the world in which her children are growing. In order to do this, she should be interested in educational

advancement and worthwhile endeavors in her community.

One of her own expressions of community-mindedness was her eight years of service as a hospital volunteer, a "Pink Lady."

When Spencer divided the Mexican Mission, Camilla had opportunity to accompany him back to the nation of her birth.

Brother Joseph Bentley was to be installed as the president of the new North Mexican Mission

with headquarters at Monterrey. We drove with
the Pratts, starting out from El Paso at seven P.M.,
arriving at Chihuahua City at two A.M. after a
hazardous ride. Up at seven A.M. again, we drove
another long, hot, hard trip to Monterrey, arriving at eleven P.M. We spent two days holding
meetings with missionaries and the two branch
congregations in Monterrey.

Leaving the hotel at six A.M. on Friday, we
drove with President Bowman straight through to
Mexico City. The first part of the journey was
through tropical jungle, and for 150 miles the
road wound over a high mountain range with
precipitous gorges hundreds of feet below, a peri-
lous road to travel at high speed. We were mighty
thankful to arrive at the mission home safely.
(President Bowman was later killed in a car accident in Mexico.) The men held many meetings in
the area around Mexico City.

Later, in Chihuahua City, Brother and Sister
Pratt and Spencer took off from the airport in
Brother Pratt's small plane to fly over the mountains to Matachic, a small Mexican branch high in
the Sierra Madre mountains. Brother and Sister
Bentley and I took off with a Mexican pilot in
another small plane. Sister Bentley and I sat on
the rear seats. She was terrified and clung to me as
if her life depended on it. Every time the plane
bounced in an air pocket as it did frequently, she
closed her eyes, gasped, and clung tighter. She
hadn't wanted to go but felt it her duty.

The pilot had never been over this country
before, and when we came to the right valley he
flew around until he spotted the Pratt's plane in a

At general conference, October 1947

grassy field tethered to a fence. We landed on the
bumpy ground and tied up beside the other
plane, like horses to a hitching post.

A Mexican member was waiting for us in a
truck and we took off across the country over a
cow trail, up and down steep banks and through
sand washes, hanging to the truck for dear life.
We arrived at the church a half hour late for the
meeting. A good crowd had assembled, and on
the front row were about twenty-five boys and
girls ten to twelve years of age. After the meeting,
going back to the planes, Sister Pratt drove the
truck so that the three women could sit in the seat,

and the men stood up behind. She couldn't get it into high gear, so we chugged along in second.

For the flight back, the three men went in the Pratt plane and the three women went with the Mexican pilot. Big black storm clouds were gathering, but it seemed as if a clear corridor opened up for us to pass through. There was a constant prayer on my lips, and I'm sure the others were praying also. Sister Bentley continued to cling to me all through the hour and a half flight.

Despite her support for his work, there were times Camilla felt lonely and needed reassurance from Spencer. When he was traveling in Canada she poured out in a letter her mixed feelings:

> ... Sometimes I almost feel in the press of your many responsibilities that I don't matter very much any more. Anyone who thinks being the wife of one of the general authorities is a bed of roses should try it once, shouldn't they? Theoretically I realize and appreciate all the blessings and advantages, but sometimes I selfishly feel it would be nice not to have to share my husband with a million others. I do love and appreciate you, dear, and admire your sterling qualities. I wouldn't have you be one whit less valiant in the pursuit of your duty, ... but it is comforting to be reassured once in a while that you realize I am standing by....

In 1947 Spencer and Golden Buchanan began to work out a placement program for Indian children, whereby they could live with Latter-day Saint families during the school year to gain a good education, and return to their homes in the summer. Helen John, a Navajo girl who had precipitated the matter by asking for a place to stay during the school term so she could go to school, was the first one. The Buchanans took her into their home in Richfield, Utah. But when they received a call to oversee the missionary work among the Indians, Helen needed a place to stay while she finished beautician training in Salt Lake City. She came to live with the Kimballs. Camilla found her being there no special burden, since she helped at home as a family member would.

In May 1948 Spencer and Golden Buchanan were touring the Southwest Indian Mission when their car stuck in drifted sand. Spencer pushed and ran, pushed and ran, repeatedly straining to the utmost. That night in Phoenix an agonizing pain struck him down, clutching at his chest; he sweat profusely. But after a while the worst pain passed and he said nothing, intent on finishing the tour. Day after day he pushed on with the tour, not sparing himself. When he confided his problem to President Buchanan, word passed back to the Quorum of the Twelve. They sent him a message, "Slow down," but he seemed not to know how.

When the tour ended and he returned home, Camilla first learned of the problem. She was upset that Spencer had not let her know immediately, and fearful at the meaning of it all. He had always been so strong. Except for a terrible siege of boils, he had not been seriously ill in thirty years. Now Spencer suffered from extreme lethargy, wholly unlike him. She was beside herself, wanting to help, but finding him resistant to going to a doctor. She insisted on his having an examination; he felt so weak that he agreed, and the electrocardiogram documented serious damage done

by the heart attack. The doctor prescribed a month of
rest, but despite Camilla's protestations Spencer resolved to say nothing to other Church leaders and just
go on about his business, being careful. He was sure he
could get by. His next stake conference assignment, in
Idaho, found him feeling heavy with pain and frightened, wishing he had followed the doctor's advice.
This time when he returned home he went to bed and
stayed there even though he felt relatively well. After
four days, in the middle of the night, he awoke with the
severe pains of another heart attack. He woke Camilla
but resisted her urging that she call an ambulance. She
could do little but worry. When the worst passed he
spent the remaining hours of the night discussing with
her funeral plans and family finances, in case he
should die.

When dawn broke, the brightness of a new day
gave them hope. It appeared he would not die, at least
not just yet. After a few days more, however, Spencer
sank into depression over his condition. He already
felt inadequate, and now he could not begin to carry
his share of the load. Camilla tended him continually,
encouraging him, cheering him, and making him comfortable.

When he had recovered somewhat, after seven
weeks, Spencer went alone to the Navajo reservation
for convalescence of two weeks in the high pines.
When he returned he immediately began to work
again and in a few days the heavy pains returned.
Camilla hurriedly packed their suitcases and they
caught a train for Long Beach, where they sought out a
quiet apartment facing the ocean. There on some days
they went through the physical and psychological torture of hours of unrelieved pain and concern that

death might be imminent. They went over plans for funeral and family arrangements and handling of property and so on. At other times Spencer felt much better. Camilla took care of shopping, cooking, cleaning, running errands, waiting on Spencer "hand and foot." Pains recurred but were not linked to any particular exertion, so it was difficult to know what to do. Weeks passed and Camilla struggled with Spencer. He was difficult to deal with, fretting at the inactivity, worried about the work left to others, but she knew he had to be patient.

Finally he insisted on returning to Salt Lake City and gradually to work; soon he was pushing full speed ahead again. A year after his first heart attack, Spencer set out on another tour of the Southwest Indian Mission. Camilla wrote him: "Dearest, I can count off two days of the thirty you will be gone! That isn't much and I am not looking forward without some dread of the long, lonesome time. I do miss you, so very much. I can't quite get over the terror that you are reenacting the tragedy of a year ago, and while I know I shouldn't suggest the possibility of a repetition, I do hope you will exercise judgment and not take chances. You are so recreant about caring for yourself."

Heart pains came back in 1949, severe enough to force Spencer to leave the city, since if he stayed he could not well avoid interviews and involvement with people's problems. On December 30 Camilla and Spencer drove south to Pima. At the Eyring farm Spencer lounged for two weeks in pajamas or old clothes. Some nights he lay in his bed starkly awake through hour upon hour of agony; there was nothing Camilla could do to help, so she just suffered along with him.

Picnic at Mt. Graham, Arizona, 1952: Edward Eyring, Edward Kimball, Caroline Romney Eyring, Mary Eyring, Camilla

She had not spent so much time with her parents in thirty years, she enjoyed visiting with them. They had grown old. Her father was eighty, her mother seventy-five, but they were still much the same. Her father was a quiet, kindly person, always gentle and unassuming, easy to be with. Her mother was a busy person, anxious that everything possible should be done for their comfort. Camilla gathered strength and support from them in this time of stress.

Spencer underwent more tests and they looked for a doctor who could offer relief; it proved a long, frustrating convalescence. Camilla suffered vicariously all the pains and had her own worries about how to keep Spencer from being depressed about his condition and how to keep him from overtaxing himself.

As though to tax her endurance and Spencer's, in

1950 Spencer's voice became hoarse and the hoarseness hung on and deepened. Finally Dr. Cowan diagnosed the new problem as possible cancer of the vocal cords. Keeping their worries to themselves, Spencer and Camilla did not tell even their children. They would not breathe the dread word *cancer* until they had to. Spencer submitted to a painful biopsy; analysis of the slides showed that it was not cancer, but an infection which needed cauterization. He received a priesthood blessing and put off the operation. The infection then healed without treatment and his voice regained its strength. They felt especially grateful for this blessing—Spencer's voice seemed so essential to his work.

Camilla's mother became ill with stomach cancer early in 1954. Camilla brought her from Arizona to Salt Lake City by airplane for treatment, and she stayed for some time with her sisters Rose and Caroline. When it appeared no treatment could help, Camilla took her mother into her home and put her in the master bedroom. Though she suffered intense nausea and had great discomfort, Camilla's mother never complained, but kept up a cheerful manner. She was nearly eighty and sensed that she would die soon. She said to one of the children, "I'm glad Papa and Emma will have some time by themselves. Anyway, I guess I'm glad." When it appeared that nothing more could be done for her, she simply stopped eating. Camilla and the rest of the family agreed that it would be cruel to try to prolong her life by heroic means. She suffered and lost strength but not her composure. The last night, as she was cared for in Camilla's home, the doctor came to check on her. He asked, "How are you today, Sister Eyring?" She roused herself through the pain and drugs to say, weakly, "I'm fine, just fine." The doctor said to the family, "She knows she is going to die, yet she is always cheerful and uncomplaining."

I cannot think of Mother without remembering her complete unselfishness. When she fixed a meal, the best must be for Papa, all others must be cared for, and then whatever seemed least desired by others or what was left over was the portion she wanted for herself. The poverty of her youth made her extremely thrifty. To see any least thing wasted was abhorrent to her. Her life was one long service to others. She was completely loyal to family, community, church, and church leaders. Faultfinding was a sin in her eyes, and she refused to listen to gossip or scandal. Having sacrificed so much and worked so hard all her life, she had little patience with those who seemed to complain, when by comparison they had so much. She couldn't help being impatient with anyone slow or lazy. I never remember seeing her sit down to rest without something in her hands to do, and speed was a virtue to her.

Mother never complained about her situation, but I sensed it was hard for her to share her husband. In some ways it was easier and in other ways harder to share him with her sister. She could not turn to her own parents for any sympathy, but on the other hand the sisters loved one another and shared values and background. When Spencer and I came to visit Mother we always stopped in to see Aunt Emma, but Mother would sometimes say, a little plaintively, "Don't stay very long."

I have nothing but admiration for people such as Father, Mother, and Aunt Emma, who are able to put aside their selfishness to live a demanding principle like plural marriage. Father's practice was strict equality, providing alike for his two families. At the end of the week he would pack his bag and move, no matter what. Of course, for most of the time the families lived side by side, so he was involved with them continually.

I know that plural marriage was a great trial to my mother, though she said little about it. No one was kinder to me than Aunt Emma. Her children were my brothers and sisters too, yet I never knew them quite as well as my own mother's children. Of course, Tony, the oldest of Aunt Emma's children to survive, was only six when I left home, so I did not have the long, close association with them that I would have had if I had not gone away at seventeen.

Three of Camilla's brothers and sisters had died in infancy, but this was the first death in her family for nearly fifty years. She felt a great loss. She and her mother had always been close. Caroline Eyring was a loving, understanding person, whose complete unselfishness Camilla came to appreciate more and more as time passed.

In December 1956 Camilla went with Spencer to a stake conference in Thatcher, Arizona.

As we reached the Kaibab Forest in northern Arizona we found snow and the roads icy in stretches. About four miles south of Jacob's Lake we came to the top of a sharp decline and saw ahead a diesel truck stalled on the road. It couldn't make the upgrade because of the ice. The driver was out throwing gravel under his wheels. We began the descent slowly, hoping we could pass the truck safely, but just before we came upon it, we began to skid, and it was apparent we would hit. We were going so slowly that we didn't anticipate real disaster. Like the proverbial ostrich, I closed my eyes and braced for the collision. It came with a bang, throwing me to the floor of the car. I must have been thrown with my back against the door handles. It knocked my breath out, and I felt sure I was dying; I gasped a breath and then blacked out a second and third time, each time having that sinking, crushing feeling of oblivion. I remembered reading that there is less danger if one stays with the car in case of accident, so I was hanging tenaciously to the seat as I sat crumpled on the floor. I had the sensation of falling through space, though I had not seen the car cross the highway and make a nose-dive down a fifty-foot embankment to come to rest against a tree at the bottom of the canyon. The pain was terrific, and it was impossible to get a real breath. Spencer thought I was screaming for fear, and said, "Well, Mama, I guess we are all right," and I answered, "No, I am dying." He wanted to lift me up onto the seat, but I was sure it would be the end of me if I were moved, for I felt crushed in the middle.

A group of eight men quickly gathered, and after prying the front bumper off the wheel, they were finally able to push the car along the side of the canyon onto an old road. I was fearful we were going to tip over and go down the canyon to finish our destruction.

Spencer and one of the men succeeded in lifting me onto the seat, and I was grateful to find that my legs were not broken. With the help of a road grader, we were pulled up onto the side of the main road, out of the way. Someone notified the Arizona Highway Patrol, and Spencer asked them to send for an ambulance and doctor from Kanab. He and one of the men who had stopped to help prayed for me. Every breath was excruciating pain, and I didn't suffer in silence.

While we waited for help to come, Spencer found some aspirin in the bag and gave me a couple of tablets and some snow to satisfy my intense thirst. We waited one and a half hours until the patrol finally came and took record of the accident, but they didn't offer any help. Then Spencer decided to see if we could cripple up to Jacob's Lake. The brake was clamped on and the fender was dragging the wheel, but we finally made it to the service station, only to find that no one was interested in helping. There was no ambulance in Kanab, and no doctor was coming, so we limped along the thirty more miles to Kanab and the hospital there. They brought a wheelchair and I managed to get onto it. Examination indicated that I no doubt had broken ribs, although there was nothing critical.

This all happened on Camilla's sixty-second birthday. She reminded Spencer what an unusual birthday party he was giving her. She also insisted that he should go on to his conference in St. Joseph Stake, which he could do by taking a bus at three A.M. The local stake president came to the hospital, and he and Spencer administered to her.

> I was fairly comfortable with the help of seda-
> tives except when I tried to move. I screamed
> plenty. I am sorry for the nurses and the other
> patients, for I really made a fuss.

While she was in the hospital many local Church leaders and others came to comfort her, and telegrams, telephone calls, and letters began to pour in. Spencer phoned every day he was gone. On December 13, just a week after they had left home, Camilla began the journey back to Salt Lake City in a station wagon that their son-in-law, Grant, brought. They made a bed in the back for Camilla, but the trip home was still arduous for her.

In the X rays taken at the LDS Hospital in Salt Lake City doctors found four breaks in her ribs on the right side and an accumulation of fluid in her punctured lung.

Four days later she was released from the hospital. Olive Beth, who always came to her rescue, arrived the next day to finish Camilla's Christmas shopping, though she was to deliver her sixth child soon. She brought Stephen, who was just getting over Bright's disease, and her youngest, eighteen months old. Spencer, who was working at home and looking after Camilla, took full responsibility for the two little children that day. He had not done that for a long time. At 7:30, when Olive Beth returned, she was in labor. Camilla provided her with a nightgown and toiletries and Spencer took her directly to the hospital. The baby arrived less than thirty minutes after they arrived. When Grant called Camilla to find out whether she knew where his wife and children were, he learned that he had a new son.

Over the next few days, despite ribs that hurt at every move, Camilla helped care for Olive Beth's three youngest children, made Christmas candy, and managed with some help to feed twenty-three of her descendants at her home for Christmas and New Year celebrations.

10

After Camilla's mother died, her father and Aunt Emma moved to Mesa to be near the Arizona Temple. He had grown too old for farming and she for her work in the post office, and they wanted to do ordinance work for their deceased relatives. In April Father Eyring wrote to his son Henry: "We are still ailing very badly. Emma is suffering so badly with her back she has a steel brace now but still the pain goes on. Can't complain, no pain, plenty to eat, and good sleep. What more do I want?"

A few days later he died, almost ninety years old. His large family gathered to pay this gentle patriarch tribute before he was buried beside his wife Caroline in the Pima cemetery, where he was joined a few months later by his second wife, Emma. These three exemplified throughout their lives a deep commitment to the marriage they had undertaken. Vernon Romney, brother to Caroline and Emma, once said that he loved all his sisters very much; these strong-willed Romney women were wonderful people, but he wouldn't be married to one of them for anything. And he marveled at Ed Eyring's courage in marrying two of them.

That Caroline and Emma were willing to share Ed Eyring as a husband said a great deal for him, and that the three of them maintained their harmonious marriage, with the dedication and self-sacrifice that entailed, said a great deal for them all.

Even before her father's death, Camilla had become worried about Spencer's throat. His voice became hoarse again after about five years in remission. When the hoarseness grew worse, Dr. Cowan ordered another biopsy of tissue from the vocal cord. This time the biopsy, which itself took away Spencer's voice for weeks, showed malignancy that required surgery. The specialist prescribed removal of all the vocal cords, but Spencer deemed his voice essential to his work, and after consultation with President McKay and Elder Harold B. Lee, he persuaded the surgeon to leave a part of one cord so that there might be hope of a little sound.

As with the heart attacks, Camilla's role was to stand by and suffer vicariously, to give encouragement when Spencer felt depressed, to nurse him in his recovery, and to be there, always be there. Spencer wrote to a friend, "I have had two hectic weeks, rugged ones. . . . Camilla has been an angel through it all." He knew he had someone special for a companion.

Earlier, at a missionary meeting, he said he had brought his wife for the missionaries to meet because she represented a mark the young men could aim for. He told the elders, "Marry someone better than you are. I would never be in the Council of the Twelve today if I had married some of the girls that I have known. Sister Kimball kept me growing and never let me be satisfied with mediocrity." In his journal he wrote, "How glad I was to have her . . . by my side! She is so strong and splendid! How I love her!" And again, "She is very pretty and looks very well in red. She is a

Camilla at Isla Patrulla, Uruguay, 1959

lovely lady and she adds so much to my peace and well being."

She sustained his spirits through the long, silent weeks and rejoiced with him when, with great difficulty, he developed a new voice and resumed his work.

In late 1960 Spencer received an assignment to visit missions and stakes in Australia and New Zealand along with a delegation of officers of the general Church auxiliaries. Between the numerous conferences the group had a chance to see some of the country.

Perhaps the most unusual bit of sightseeing was our visit to Waitomo Caves. As we started down the steep steps to the mouth of the glowworm cave, I slipped on the stair and injured my leg painfully. I was determined not to miss this sight, for my brother Henry had been so impressed by it, so I crawled down the rest of the stairs and into the boat. We floated quietly around the cave on the lake, which fills the large grotto. On the ceiling are thousands of glow worms with their lights shining in the darkness. They look like tiny stars or electric lights.

Despite her painful leg, Spencer and Camilla decided to travel on around the world. From Australia they flew to Singapore, where Spencer visited government officials concerning the possibility of sending missionaries there.

We walked down the bank of the Singapore River for many blocks. The river is full of Chinese junks carrying cargo. It is an open sewer and filthy beyond description. This was Christmas Eve, but no outward semblance of the Christian celebration was evident.

On Christmas Day they flew to Saigon, Vietnam, arriving there around noon.

The costume of the Vietnamese women consists of long trousers with wide legs if they are from the south, and narrow legs if from the north of the country. Over the trousers flows a dress with high neck and long sleeves usually made of sheer material, and the skirt is slit on each side clear to the waist so that it billows in the breeze. Their hats are cone-shaped straw. I purchased a

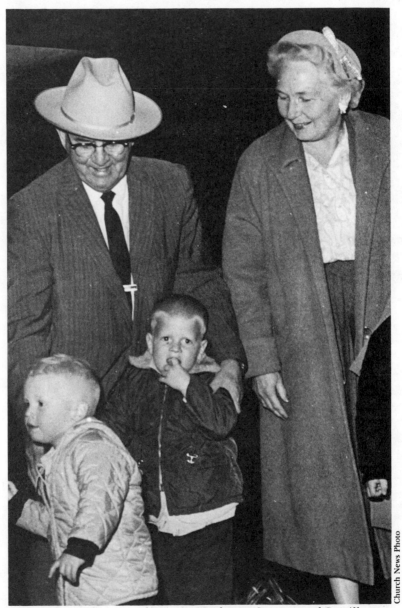

Grandsons Thomas and Spencer Mack greet Spencer and Camilla at airport

nice one for one dollar. There were some Christmas decorations in the hotel lobby, but it was hard to get the Christmas spirit. I read the Christmas story from Luke and from Third Nephi before going to bed.

On New Year's Day Camilla wrote in Calcutta, India:

The scene from our hotel window is a most distressing one, even though it is in the best part of the city center. A family has set up living on the sidewalk across a narrow back street. They slept all night in filthy rags. This morning I saw a tiny baby push its head out from under the rags by the mother's head. There is a constant flow of poverty-stricken humanity. Many two-wheeled carts pulled by running men serve for transportation. People were washing themselves and drinking from a street hydrant. It began to rain and drizzled all afternoon. People tried to find shelter in doorways. We fasted and spent the day mostly in our room reading and resting.

January 2. We took a guided tour of the city. The sacred cows roam the streets leaving their droppings, which are quickly salvaged and pasted by hand on walls and tree trunks and, when dried, sold for fuel. To treat cows so seems a senseless custom to us who are of other faiths and cultures.

January 3. On our way to breakfast we passed through a patio and a big fat rat ran directly across our way. It was a shock. In the afternoon we flew to Benares, where we stayed at the Clark Hotel, eighty years old, but a nice resort type. Our beds

Left, in the Valley of the Kings, Egypt, January 1961. Below, standing before the Mount of Olives.

were fitted with net canopies to keep out mos-
quitoes and other bugs. We rode in a boat up the
Ganges River and saw the human bodies pushed
off the platform into the sacred river to be de-
voured by the fish—saints, children under five,
lepers, and smallpox victims thus buried—and
saw people drinking the water. Why don't they
die? The guide said it was because the water was
sacred. As we passed through the throng of filthy
beggars, sick, lame, and starving, and the weeping
widows hopelessly wailing in their lone dwellings,
I began to cry, completely overcome. It took all my
will power to keep from having hysterics.

Camilla's leg continued to pain her, but she had no
intention of letting it interfere with seeing these new
places.

Their journey onward included Pakistan, Syria,
Iran, Egypt, Israel, Greece, Italy, and Spain. Where
they could, they contacted members of the Church,
who always gave them a warm welcome. People who
lived so far from Church headquarters seemed especially appreciative of their visit.

Of all the places they went, the one that moved
Camilla most was the Garden Tomb, where Christ may
have been laid. In this quiet place few people came that
winter day to disturb their meditations. They sat,
wrapped in scarves against the chill but warmed by the
January sun, reading the scriptures to one another.
They stayed and stayed and knelt together in solemn
prayer of gratitude that they knew the Lord and were
beneficiaries of his atonement.

In Rome distances between points of interest were
too near to justify a taxi and too far to walk, but walk

Fiftieth anniversary trip to Mexico with children and spouses, 1967:
Spencer, Andrew, Evelyn, Phyllis, Camilla, Edward, Spencer LeVan,
Kathryn, Olive Beth, Grant Mack

they did—miles and miles, despite Camilla's painful leg. She did it from choice, to save the money.

The year 1967 marked fifty years of marriage. Looking back, it all seemed to have passed so quickly. Their four children were all well settled. LeVan (called Spence now) was professor of law at the University of Michigan; Olive Beth had started to teach school in Salt Lake City because of her husband's failing eyesight; Andrew planned international marketing for General Electric at its New York headquarters; Edward was professor of law at the University of Wisconsin. Each was happily married. Among them they provided Camilla and Spencer with twenty-seven grandchildren.

Golden wedding anniversary, 1967

Camilla and Spencer wanted to do something spectacular for this fiftieth wedding anniversary. Even with only four children it had been twenty years since all had been together at once. They invited the four children with their spouses to join them in a summer trip to Mexico, where for ten days they explored the ruins, feasted, swam in the Pacific, and spent more time in relaxed visiting than they had ever been able to do before. Then near Christmas time the children responded by bringing together thirty-six of the thirty-nine family members for a more formal celebration of the golden wedding anniversary. Spencer wrote in his journal that the children "seem to like to come home. We are getting paid well now for any sacrifice we made."

Camilla had over the years proven a faithful correspondent. Children away from home could expect a weekly letter, usually written on Sunday, telling of family news and reiterating her love. She remembered with a note and a gift all the birthdays of all the family members.

When the children left home she released them gracefully, having reared them to be independent like herself. She loved them, but did not need them to keep her life full.

Camilla managed to keep from interfering with her married children's decisions and even refrained from expressing strong opinions, though she often had to bite her lip. But when Grant proposed that he and Olive Beth might move to Alaska, Camilla came to the breaking point. She said, with restraint but strong feeling, "Make awfully sure this is the right thing to do. Surely you wouldn't want to do that to me!" To have her only daughter move so far away seemed just too much.

Camilla kept her ties with her children tight by her unfailing loyalty. They could almost always count on her to be there when they performed in plays or concerts, football or basketball games. And she liked to support her grandchildren the same way. She cheered her grandsons in all sports but wrestling. She watched one wrestling match and was so sure her grandson was going to be permanently injured that she could not stand to watch any more.

When a granddaughter had responsibility for a fund-raising activity for a new chapel, Camilla agreed to give a book review for a dollar a ticket. Another time she substituted for a sick granddaughter in giving a Relief Society lesson.

Camilla and Spencer took many of their grandchildren with them on train trips before the youngsters turned old enough to require a ticket. And the grandchildren sometimes joined them on vacations. In 1971 two of them helped Camilla pick wild blackberries near Santa Cruz, California, and make jam. Then, when it was time to leave, Camilla had them help clean the apartment until it was cleaner than when they had rented it.

She took great satisfaction in all her children's and grandchildren's accomplishments, but especially in their Church activities. It gave her particular pleasure that her children and most of her grandchildren married in the temple and many of them filled missions and otherwise gave service in the Church. The inactivity of some of her family caused her deep grief, but it did not diminish her love. One letter to her reflected awareness of her feelings; reporting an academic honor, it said, a bit apologetically, "I know you'd much rather that I'd been made president of the elders quorum."

Camilla had church, friends, books, handwork, and gardening to keep her days busy. She did beautiful handwork—embroidering, crocheting, needlepoint, tatting, and cutwork, and covered dozens of benches, chairs, and footstools with her needlepoint. She made many gifts of cutwork waterlily embroi-

Church News Photo

Church News Photo

dered sheet and pillow slip sets, painstaking in their workmanship.

She also genuinely loved gardening. In her city lot vegetables grew among the roses, beans climbed to the

With grandchildren Joseph, Miles, Sarah, Jordan, and Mary Kimball, 1974

Church News Photo

roof of her porch, and fruit trees shaded her yard. Canning the produce extended the satisfaction she had in living from the labor of her own hands. Lilacs, delphiniums, tulips, petunias, and especially roses grew in joyful profusion from spring to fall. She wore a broad hat to keep her fair skin from burning, and poured her sweat into digging and weeding and trimming.

The fiftieth anniversary provided occasion for major celebration, but on their next anniversary Spencer wrote in his journal, "Today is our fifty-first wedding anniversary...both of us forgot." He reflected on their "fifty-one years of glorious married life, and how grateful I am for a companion of such stature and strength and kindness and affection."

When in 1968 Spencer received an assignment to

the Juarez Stake conference in northern Mexico, he invited Camilla, their daughter, Olive Beth, and Camilla's sister Mary to accompany him. Camilla and Mary had not been back to Colonia Juarez since they left in 1912.

> As soon as we were settled, we set out on a walking tour of the little town. The little house where Mary and I were born is still standing, a small red brick home with a porch across the front. Memories came rushing back. What fun it was to relive my childhood experiences!
>
> Grandma Eyring's house was gone. The old church and schoolhouse had been remodeled, and there were other major changes, but many landmarks remained.
>
> Sister Brown, the stake president's wife, took us over the old dusty road to Pearson, where we had taken the train fifty-six years before as refugees. A train passed through while we were there, making the memories even more vivid.

11

Camilla had had many worries and heartaches over Spencer's health, starting with smallpox the first year of their marriage and continuing through boils, heart attacks, and throat cancer. In 1971 matters came to a crisis again. For some time Spencer had become progressively weaker. It got to the point that he could not walk a block without resting. He was so unutterably fatigued that each time he exerted himself Camilla feared disaster. Tests showed that a defective heart valve and nearly clogged cardiac arteries threatened total heart failure at any time. He needed open heart surgery and any delay meant increasing the risk. But at the same time Dr. Cowan discovered a new cancerous spot on Spencer's poor remnant of a vocal cord. This double blow seemed as if it might be the beginning of the end.

With this discouraging prospect, they sought a priesthood blessing. Camilla received comfort from a blessing under the hands of President Harold B. Lee.

It gave me more feeling of strength and peace than I had had for a long time. I realized that I had given up hope and was allowing myself to be morbid and defeated. I tried doubly hard to be cheerful and hopeful, though I continued to have my dark moments when the tears and anguish found vent.

The first step was to treat the cancer, since there seemed no point in the heart surgery unless the cancer could be removed by surgery or radiation. Further surgery on his larynx could mean only silence, so Spencer and Camilla opted for six weeks of radiation treatment. Though the twenty-four cobalt treatments reduced his voice to a whisper for a time, the radiation finally proved successful in destroying the cancer. They then faced the prospect of a surgeon's opening the chest cavity, prying the ribs apart, and invading the heart to install a metal and plastic mechanical valve as well as to shunt the blood past two obstructions in arteries. The alternative was progressive decline and death. The operation had been performed on so few men of Spencer's age that estimating his chances of survival constituted only rough guesswork, but Dr. Russell Nelson, who would perform the surgery, thought it might be seventy-five percent. Spencer insisted on postponing the operation until after April general conference, so he could get his affairs in order and not miss conference.

As the time approached, Camilla felt under great tension. She worried to herself about the outcome, but the reality of God and the efficacy of prayer and faith and priesthood administration sustained and comforted her. "How else could I have carried on?"

The decision to proceed had been made only in consultation with the First Presidency, and in preparation for the operation Spencer received a special administration from his brethren in the temple. Camilla also received another blessing from Elder Marion G. Romney.

The operation began early in the morning. Camilla, with two of her children, waited through the four and a half hours of suspense.

> I was surprised that I took it as calmly as I did. I shed only a few tears. Somehow after the blessing at the temple I felt all would be well. We had a long vigil, but fortunately Dr. Homer Ellsworth went into the operating room periodically and kept us posted. The crucial point was when the heart took over on its own after the repair work was done. The heart had not been functioning for one hour and fifty-five minutes.

Then came the period of slow recovery. No time in Spencer's life had been as miserable as the following weeks, more from the excruciating pain in his tortured ribs, with every breath, than from the heart operation itself. While he was in intensive care, Camilla stayed by his side as much as she was allowed. Then when he was moved to a separate room she slept in the room with him, on a cot, where she would be constantly available. As he lay in bed, often groggy with medication, he liked to have Camilla hold his hand. "It is hard to see him suffer," she noted. Worst of all was the coughing that therapists forced in order to keep his lungs clear. One day Olive Beth stayed with him while Camilla rushed out to fulfill a commitment to give a book review. Camilla wrote:

> For five days of his suffering I have managed to keep quite calm, but when I see him so weak

and miserable, nauseated and with cold hands as
he is today, I can't seem to hold my courage so
well. He vomited and was white and clammy. The
doctor said this often happens. Nothing seems to
surprise the doctors....

Tuesday, April 18. Up at 6:00. Spencer
seemed to feel some better. I went home at 6:30.
Had a bath, made some phone calls, and went
back to the hospital at 8:00. I parked the car on
7th Avenue, locked it, and suddenly realized that
in my haste I had locked the keys inside with the
lights on and windshield wipers operating, for it
was snowing hard. A young woman came driving
by and I hailed her. She took me down to the
Conoco station on South Temple where a good
friend of Spencer's, Brother Belliston, is the operator. He and one of his employees brought me to
the hospital, opened the car, and took the car to be
inspected and serviced; they later brought it back
and returned the keys. I have seldom been so
frustrated and embarrassed to do such a stupid
thing. I couldn't help crying a little when I had to
ask for help.

Spencer ate a fair breakfast but has been feeling very depressed and frustrated. He ate very
little for lunch. It is so hard to get any rest in a
hospital. Someone comes in every few minutes for
some reason or for no reason at all.

Camilla tried tactfully to limit the visits from family
and friends. One time Spencer said to her with tears in
his eyes, "No matter how much I love people, visiting
with them takes all my strength."

In a few hours at a time at home she did the

washing, put up strawberry preserves, and checked
the mail and paid the bills. Finally, after thirteen days
she was allowed to take Spencer home for convalescence.

The General Authorities visited faithfully.

> About 5:30 President and Sister Lee came and
> visited quite a little while. Spencer asked Brother
> Lee about the advisability of having frequent
> blessings from the brethren. Brother Lee's answer
> was that he had said to the authorities he felt
> "Spencer lives from blessing to blessing." So he
> gave Spencer a blessing, reassuring him of the
> love of Heavenly Father and of the brethren and
> of his feeling that the Lord has a mission for
> Spencer yet to fulfill. One of Spencer's greatest
> enemies is the feeling of discouragement and fear
> that plagues him because of the weakness and
> pain he continues to suffer. We have reread the
> blessing Brother Lee gave Spencer in the temple
> before he went into the hospital and have taken
> renewed courage from it.

After nearly a month Spencer for the first time
enjoyed a few minutes at a time of freedom from pain.
And though the recovery was slow, he began to regain
strength and felt a renewed zest for life. So did
Camilla.

They went to Laguna Beach, California, to con-
valesce, staying in the home the Church owned. While
they were there, President and Sister Lee came to stay
with them for two nights. Even though Camilla had
known President Lee for thirty years, she wrote:

I was worried about fixing the right food, but they were very appreciative. Sister Lee insisted on helping with the dishes and all. This was a great honor to have a counselor in the First Presidency stay with us.

Two weeks later, in July 1972, President Joseph Fielding Smith died quietly, suddenly, and Harold B. Lee succeeded him as president of the Church; Spencer became president of the Council of the Twelve. Though he still lacked strength, Spencer began increasing the amount of work he insisted on doing. Camilla scolded a little, but she knew he had to feel he was giving his best to the important calling.

Then a few months later the tables turned. Camilla felt chagrined at finding herself a hospital patient for the first time in fifty years, losing her appendix at age seventy-seven.

> I went to the clinic and the white cell count had risen to 11,000, so Dr. Wilkinson directed me to LDS Hospital at once. I already had my bag in the car, because I thought I might need it. I did not want to disturb Spencer yet, so in spite of the pain I drove to the hospital, parked in the parking lot, and walked alone to the emergency entrance, where I was admitted. They then called Spencer, who was in meeting, and told him that I was going into an emergency operation for appendicitis.
>
> The most traumatic aspect was that I was to give the Relief Society spiritual living lesson on November 1, the day I was admitted to the hospital. There was nothing I could do but just drop it in the lap of Sister Conover, the Relief Society president. She called Sister Haglund, who gives the lesson in the First Ward, and she carried on. Everyone has said how very well she did. I didn't get one bit of consolation that I was missed at all. It is good for one to be reminded that she is not indispensable. This whole experience has taken good care of that. The world has gone smoothly on its way with no concern that I haven't been on the job.

The appendix had perforated, so the operation was a true emergency. When the day arrived for her to go home from the hospital, her doctor noticed pus and drainage from Camilla's wound, but he allowed her to go home anyway, thinking she would recover just as well there. Later on in the day, all alone, she became very worried over new pain and drainage, so when the president of the ward Relief Society called, Camilla tearfully asked for help. The president and her counselor, a nurse, came immediately and reassured her that the condition was not unusual and that she would live. Then Spencer came home and her worst fears vanished.

> Spencer has been most kind and thoughtful. This has not been easy for him, added to his own problems of health and responsibility.

The doctor started Camilla on a week-long course of antibiotics. It was a long, discouraging week because she feared that a new operation might be needed. She questioned the doctor's judgment a little, feeling that maybe she would not survive the waiting game he was playing.

> When I was so discouraged, Spencer asked President Marion G. Romney if he would come in the evening and give me a special blessing. He did, and as he prayed, one statement impressed me indelibly: "I bless you with the gift to be healed." It was as if those words were imprinted on a banner before me. The lesson I had spent so much time in preparing and could not give had been on "gifts of the Spirit."
>
> As I continued to contemplate this blessing, it was borne in upon me with greater and greater clarity that I had had a special blessing given at a time of greatest need and that it was up to me to

claim that blessing. It was up to me to take courage, to determine to do everything in my power that I might have the gift to be healed. I bear my testimony to this spiritual experience and feel a great responsibility to claim this blessing.

12

On December 26, 1973, Arthur Haycock called Spencer from the LDS Hospital at 8:30 P.M. and reported that President Harold B. Lee was critically ill. Spencer grabbed his coat and rushed to the hospital. He met President Romney and family members there. They could only wait and pray. So many doctors and their equipment filled the room that neither the family nor anyone else could go into it. At 8:58 President Lee was pronounced dead. At that moment responsibility for leadership of the Church shifted to Spencer as president of the Council of the Twelve.

A few minutes later a distressed call came from Spencer saying, "Pray for me. President Lee is dead." I couldn't believe it. Ever since Spencer left I had been praying so anxiously that President Lee would recover. In fact, ever since he became president of the Church, Spencer and I had prayed earnestly night and morning and in between for his protection and health. We realized that only he stood between Spencer and the fact that Spencer might become president of the Church. It is something neither of us ever desired; in fact, we had been terrified at the thought

166

*At funeral of President Harold B. Lee,
December 29, 1973*

it might come. But President Lee was four years
younger than Spencer and had never had the
serious health problems that beset Spencer. We
had every reason to believe he would outlive
Spencer.

President Lee's death shocked and grieved the
whole Church. The funeral was held in the Salt Lake
Tabernacle December 29. Spencer presided and conducted and spoke feelingly of the death of his friend.
Camilla mourned for the widow.

Rain fell intermittently, and during the ceremony at the cemetery it came in torrents. I stood
beside Sister Lee, who naturally is overcome with

grief. The death was so sudden and so completely unexpected. My heart goes out to her.

The next day the apostles met in the temple at three o'clock for a long meeting, and sustained Spencer as the twelfth president of the Church.

The thought of the tremendous responsibility is overwhelming. The complexity of the position becomes more and more apparent, and I am sometimes filled with anxiety. But I feel confident that the Lord will give the needed help and that Spencer will fill this position with honor and effectiveness as he has every responsibility that has come to him. The people churchwide love him, and supporting letters, telegrams, and telephone messages have flooded in.

The public scrutiny that had always been difficult for Camilla multiplied ten times at once. The routine of their lives changed drastically, and sometimes in unexpected ways. During general conference the next April, when Spencer was to be sustained as president by the membership of the Church, they were asked to stay at the Hotel Utah for security reasons, because threats had been made against the president. A security man sat in the hallway outside their room all night, and anyone authorized to come to the door knocked four times and gave the password, "Cumorah." It was disconcerting for Camilla to be forced out of her home, even for a few days. It was a little like being a refugee again. When they returned home, surveillance continued.

> This is beginning to get on my nerves. I woke
> up at two A.M. when two security men were chang-
> ing shifts. We had left the bedroom door partly
> ajar, and I could see the two of them visiting in the
> living room. This was almost more than I could
> take. I wanted to call out and tell them to please go
> home and leave us alone. Who would have
> thought that we who love our independence and
> our privacy so much would be surrounded by
> guards?

Later the guards moved outside into a parked car, and
this restored a measure of privacy. They were sensitive
to the situation and did their best to be unobtrusive.
Spencer and Camilla came to appreciate greatly the
help and protection they provided.

Saturday, April 6, 1974, the solemn assembly convened in the Salt Lake Tabernacle. This was the fifth
solemn assembly for sustaining a new president that
Camilla had witnessed in the thirty years she had been
in Salt Lake City. Always an impressive occasion, this
solemn assembly was special. Most of their children,
grandchildren, and great-grandchildren had
gathered, as well as many of her relatives and
Spencer's. Camilla felt some anxiety, but took comfort
from the support of her family, who sat in a special
section in the north balcony. She went up and greeted
them before the session began.

As she stood with the rest of the Church to sustain
her husband as prophet, she raised her hand without
reservation. No one in the world knew better than she
that he was not perfect, but no one knew better than

Greeting Sister Nathan Eldon Tanner
in Tabernacle

she how hard he had tried through all their life
together to serve the Lord faithfully and well. He was
personally worthy of the calling, and she had a sure
conviction that the Lord had indeed called him.
"Spencer presided and conducted and spoke, all with
dignity and inspiration. I was very proud of him."

As soon as the meeting ended she hurried home to
set out the food she had been preparing for days to
feed the crowd of over a hundred friends and relatives
who would come to an open house. No one set her on a
silken pillow, nor did she want to be. She and Spencer
spent the evening busily entertaining their guests.

After some months of experience Camilla's feelings remained the same.

This responsibility which has come to Spencer to be Prophet, Seer, and Revelator of the Church puts us on a pedestal neither Spencer nor I would ever have chosen. I would much prefer a quiet, private life. But I recognize it as a great privilege, and my constant prayer is that we both may be able to fulfill our parts honorably and humbly, that our Heavenly Father and Christ will not be ashamed of us. People have been most kind in their acceptance. Everyone loves Spencer.

Some things are the same as before. Spencer was always dedicated to the Church, and it has been that way in our married life from the beginning. He was just as devoted when he was stake clerk. He cannot work any harder. The main difference is that now he is the last resort of authority on earth, and it sets him apart so. When he was an apostle, at least he could look to the First Presidency. Now he has the final responsibility for so many decisions, and there is no place for him to go except to the Lord.

I take as much responsibility as I can for his health, relieve him of the business of the house, and, yes, I try to shelter him. It is the hardest thing in the world for him to say no, and it is hard for me to see him under such pressure.

Camilla felt that her principal church job was to care for the president of the Church, to cook for him, to love him, and to protect him. She ironed his white shirts (sometimes more than one a day), washed his clothes, maintained his house, did his shopping. When a woman asked incredulously, "Do you buy your own groceries?" Camilla's slightly quizzical counter-question was, "Who do you think would buy them?" If she had felt she could afford a servant, her pride in her own independence would make it all but impossible. Even for a large party she rarely had other help than Olive Beth provided.

Women used to ask, "What is it like to be married to an apostle?" and she had answered, "Well, you know, I was married to him twenty-five years before he was one." Now they asked, "What is it like to be married to the president of the Church?" But the answer, "I was married to him fifty-six years before he was one," did not quite satisfy. It *was* different, since he occupied a unique position. Whereas previously she had to share him with others, there was now something approaching a relinquishment of him to the needs of others. She once listed some facets of her life as the president's wife:

> It is to be loved by and to live with a righteous and good man who is honest and kind.
>
> It is to have a husband so occupied with his sacred responsibilities that all else must play second fiddle to them.
>
> It is to fit housekeeping and family and personal life into the complex schedule he must keep.
>
> It is to have a husband perennially late for meals and to have the frustration of trying to keep his food fresh yet warm.
>
> It is to travel to visit the Church members around the world and feel the pulse and the love of the good people everywhere.
>
> It is to keep smiling and shaking hands with these same loving people to the point of exhaustion.

It is to lose privacy, to have guards for protection when shopping, going to a family party, or sitting quietly at home.

It is to be the housekeeper, cook, gardener, laundress, social secretary, and family liaison officer—all in one weary woman.

It is to receive hundreds of gifts that must be acknowledged as well as enjoyed, and thousands of Christmas greetings one cannot begin to respond to.

It is to be remembered in the prayers of millions of people and to sense their faith and concern.

The additional demands on her time made it difficult to keep up with all the cultural groups to which she had belonged during her years in Salt Lake City—the Alice Louise Reynolds Club, the Culture Club, Cleofan, the Daughters of Utah Pioneers, the Authors Club, and the Thetas. She began having to cut back her participation in some, though she enjoyed the women who belonged and the intellectual stimulation that came from their various programs of study.

In addition, she and Spencer regularly attended two dinner groups each month: one group that first attended a temple session together, and one that met at the Lion House for a discussion of Church history.

On the occasion of her eightieth birthday, in 1974, fifty-five of Camilla's closest relatives gathered to honor her at a beautifully appointed dinner party. A little orchestra of grandchildren played, and her brothers and sisters reminisced and paid her tribute. They reiterated their admiration for Camilla's equanimity in the face of difficulties, her sweet love

Speaking at Ricks College upon receipt of
Exemplary Womanhood Award, with
President Henry B. Eyring in background

shown to others, her intelligence and love of learning, her deep spirituality, her poise that kept people unaware of her shyness, and her willing acceptance of a role in support of her husband—encouraging, helping, honoring, and loving.

Others also recognized her praiseworthy characteristics. She received an honorary Golden Gleaner award from the YWMIA, and later both Brigham Young University and Ricks College honored her as an exemplary Latter-day Saint woman.

After Spencer became president of the Church, Camilla received many more invitations to speak. She always did her best, worrying all the while that it was not better. Most of the talks were to Relief Society or mother-daughter groups, though to many other groups as well. One month she had eleven appointments, frequently eight or ten. She always accepted on

condition that Spencer's needs would have to take
precedence, and occasionally, as when the doctor ad-
vised him to leave for a few days of rest, she had to ask
to be excused.

She often spoke about mother-daughter rela-
tionships, using herself as an example. Despite her
deep love for and dependence on Olive Beth, a "viva-
cious darling," there had been times during Olive
Beth's teenage years when they had had their differences. Their ultimate closeness, which added rich-
ness to both their lives, had resulted from patient
nurturing; it had not just happened.

She liked also to talk about Relief Society as a
worldwide sisterhood and about visiting teaching.

> I think visiting teaching is the most important
> work we do in the Church. I feel I really know a
> woman only when I enter her home. In this way I
> can serve her person-to-person. I have tried not to
> suppress any inclination to generous word or
> deed.

Camilla served as a visiting teacher for approx-
imately sixty years. She and her companions made it a
practice to go visiting teaching on the first Tuesday of
each month. But she did not visit just to fulfill an
assignment; she went to make friends.

She befriended a young mother whose husband
was not a Church member and who had herself drifted
away. Camilla finally saw her become active in the
Relief Society. Another inactive woman always received a report from Camilla on how well her children
had done when they took part in Sunday School. An
elderly woman whose husband lay ill for a long time
received frequent visits and gifts as evidence of con-

*Visiting teaching with Sister Erma Francom,
1976*

cern. Camilla and her companion faithfully called at
one woman's home month after month, even though
the woman never once answered the door, so Camilla
knew failure as well as success in the giving of Christian
service.

> The older I grow, the more I live for family
> and church. Other things grow less important in
> comparison to my relationship to the Lord and to
> his children and mine.

One time when Camilla went to speak to a Relief

Indian rug is presented to Camilla and Spencer

Society group, she was delighted to find Helen John sitting beside her on the stand and Helen's daughter introducing her. Helen had, as a young Navajo woman, lived for a time with the Kimballs. Camilla wrote:

> Our hope for the Indian nation is to educate the young people—to help them make their place in the world. It is a joy to see them overcome the docile acceptance of unhappy situations. Their tribal leaders give untiring service to better the Indian's condition. It is unfortunate that many of our own people fail to recognize the Indian as an equal. But given education and economic security, he will prove his own worth.

On another occasion she recorded:

> At our Relief Society I was asked to speak briefly about the Church Indian program. I had prepared much material but was so emotionally affected I could not control my tears. I cried all the time I talked. I feel deeply about the deprivation of these people.

Olive Beth took Arlene, a Zuni, into her home for school years between ages seven and thirteen. This pleased Camilla and Spencer, who treated Arlene as a grandchild, with full share of hugs and birthday and Christmas gifts. She called them Grandpa and Grandma. Camilla made her a pink crocheted poncho, and Arlene especially liked a shell necklace they brought her from Samoa.

In 1975 Camilla completed fourteen years as her ward's spiritual living leader. At a luncheon she received fourteen red roses in tribute for her term of devoted service. Two weeks later, with the help of her daughter and granddaughter, she served luncheon at her home for fifty-three women who had read the Doctrine and Covenants. Each year she challenged the women to read along with her the Book of Mormon, Pearl of Great Price, *Jesus the Christ,* or some other such book, or to write their life story. She rewarded those who met the challenge with lunch at her home. One year seventy-two women read the Book of Mormon. Each time many expressed appreciation for the stimulus to do what they had often put off.

A few days after the luncheon Camilla held open house for the fiancée of her grandson, as she did for every grandchild who lived in Utah, when the time of marriage approached. This time eighty guests came. (She sometimes had as many as 120 guests.) The next day she bottled twelve pints of watermelon pickles from the rind of the melons used for the open house. So much good watermelon rind could not be wasted.

13

Camilla traveled a great deal with Spencer to area conferences and building dedications in far places. But they did not travel as tourists any more. Only occasionally did she see much more than airports, hotels, chapels or rented meeting places, and whatever happened to lie on the path between. In 1975 they attended area conference in Sao Paulo, where Spencer made the exciting announcement of a temple to be built there. Flying to Paraguay, they passed over the spectacular Iguazu Falls, two and a half miles wide. Later that year they flew to Japan, Taiwan, Hong Kong, the Philippines, and Korea. In Korea they went to a museum to see some recently discovered engraven gold plates, linked together; to Camilla they seemed strongly reminiscent of the Book of Mormon plates.

In California Camilla and Spencer visited a camp of Vietnamese refugees and met with the small group of Latter-day Saints among them. Her heart went out to them. She also had been a refugee alien in a foreign land at age seventeen, though she knew that differences in language and culture made their adjustment much more difficult than hers had been.

She sometimes made cultural mistakes. On an earlier visit to the Orient two Korean women presented

Top, visiting Saints in Samoa. Bottom, dressed in Korean costume and speaking to Korean Saints, with Han In Sang translating.

her with an antique vase they spent all day selecting for her. She kissed them in appreciation, and they stiffened as though they had been struck. She asked the mission president what she had done wrong, and he explained that among Orientals it was thought inappropriate to kiss or touch in such a situation. A little later, in Japan, Camilla hugged some younger women after a meeting, without reaction, and then hugged an older woman—who reacted with shock. Camilla then remembered what she had been told in Korea. "I don't learn very fast," she said, though she tried hard to adopt the culturally accepted ways of expressing her affection.

In 1976 nine area conferences were scheduled in the Pacific. Spencer and Camilla and other Church leaders went first to Hawaii for groundbreaking of a new building on the BYU-Hawaii campus. Spencer drove the Caterpillar to move the first dirt and then several others, including Camilla, dug in with shovels. A Chinese man standing behind her said, "You're a farm girl." She felt a touch of pride in that recognition that she could handle a shovel.

They flew to American Samoa for conference first, then Western Samoa. Suddenly she and Spencer both fell ill, with temperatures of 104, nausea, coughing, and total misery. They needed help to board the airplane for New Zealand, but they insisted on going. Spencer had a television interview and a meeting with the Prime Minister scheduled immediately upon arrival, and the conference sessions had to go forward.

During the long hours of flight they slept, and then woke as they were about to land, fever broken. Spencer buttoned the collar of his damp shirt, pulled up his tie, and asked Camilla to brush his hair. She had enough sense of humor left to ask, "Which one?"

When they left the plane, they greeted the enthusiastic crowd there to welcome them, showing nothing of their illness. After the television interview and just as the luncheon with Prime Minister Muldoon was ending, Spencer's fever returned after a two-hour remission and he went immediately to bed.

In Hamilton, New Zealand, Spencer asked President N. Eldon Tanner to represent him at the cultural program planned for Saturday evening, hoping to conserve his strength for the Sunday conference sessions. But in the evening, he awakened with a start and asked Dr. Russell Nelson, who sat watching over him, "Brother Nelson, what time was that program to begin this evening?"

"At seven o'clock, President Kimball."

"What time is it now?"

"It is almost seven."

Spencer was soaked with perspiration. His fever had broken again. He said, "Tell Sister Kimball we're going."

Camilla got out of bed, and they both hurriedly dressed and then drove the short distance to the stadium where the program had just convened. President Tanner had explained at the beginning of the meeting that they were too sick to attend. In the opening prayer a young New Zealander petitioned fervently, "We three thousand New Zealand youth have gathered here prepared to sing and to dance for thy prophet. Wilt thou heal him and deliver him here." As the prayer ended, the car carrying Spencer and Camilla entered and the stadium erupted in a spontaneous, deafening shout at the answer to their prayer.

From New Zealand they flew to Fiji for the next conference. Camilla spent the day in bed. In Tonga the temperature in the auditorium was over 100 degrees and she was really very ill, yet she sat on the stand in the front row without complaint, in tangible support of her husband and the cause. She never missed a meeting in Sydney, Melbourne, or Brisbane, where the tour ended. Upon their return home, chest X rays and tests showed that they both still had viral pneumonia. The doctor prescribed medicine and rest.

The country celebrated the bicentennial of the signing of the Declaration of Independence in July, and J. Willard Marriott had arranged the Bicentennial Extravaganza at the Kennedy Center in Washington, D.C. The Tabernacle Choir performed and Spencer and Camilla sat with President and Mrs. Gerald Ford in their box, as they had on a similar occasion in 1971. Camilla found the Fords gracious hosts. The next day, Sunday, July 4, 26,000 people attended the Church commemoration of the bicentennial in Washington.

That summer proved a particularly busy one. They traveled to England and back and later to France, Finland, Denmark, the Netherlands, Germany, and Switzerland, covering tens of thousands of miles in the interests of the Church.

Spencer sometimes traveled without Camilla, but she rarely traveled anywhere without him. In 1977, however, she took a trip with her son Ed and his wife to Colonia Juarez to show them the scenes of her childhood. It proved a rewarding, sentimental journey, but she worried the whole three days she was away from Spencer.

Camilla and Spencer attended a series of area con-

ferences in Latin America. In Guatemala, part of the
cultural evening involved a dance in which one dancer
carried on his head a frame representing a bull.

> The frame was filled with firecrackers which
> boomed all over the place. One singed Sister Ken-
> nedy's eyebrow and another Sister Wilkinson's
> hair. I was really frightened that all of us on the
> front row would catch fire. One burst went off
> between Brother Perry's feet.

The next morning at the airport she was stuck with
fourteen members of their party in an elevator for a
hilarious twenty minutes. That evening in Costa Rica
she found herself stuck in an elevator for the second
time the same day.

When they met with public officials there was always picture taking. Camilla wrote, "I dread this. I
freeze a smile on my face and stand stiffly." She con-
cealed her discomfort well.

In Panama, as elsewhere in Latin America, Camilla
read her talk to the women's meeting in Spanish.

> The local women seemed to appreciate my
> efforts, though I know I made many mistakes.
> Crowds of women and children came up to kiss
> me. The security men finally whisked me away to
> a private room. I would really prefer staying with
> the women, but on advice of a nurse from the
> embassy the security people were concerned
> about my exposure to hepatitis.

The crowds of Saints who were determined to
reach and greet Spencer posed even greater problems.

In Peru, after the meeting they sang "God Be with You Till We Meet Again" and waved handkerchiefs and shed tears. Crowds lined the way out. Sometimes the crowd pressure is almost overpowering and I worry for Spencer. After we were in the bus they kept handing babies up to the window for Spencer to kiss them through the glass. The people scrambled any possible way to get to touch his hand or greet him in any way. Crowds waved as long as the bus was in sight. The love and respect the members show for the prophet touches me deeply. It is very humbling to get the reflected glory.

In Bogota, Colombia, Camilla noted with satisfaction that one of the prayers at the conference was offered by an Indian district president from Ecuador whose hair was in a braid down his back and who was wearing white linen trousers and sandals. It seemed especially fitting when Spencer spoke on the Savior's disapproval of class distinctions.

In 1977 at the BYU Women's Conference, Camilla received the first Exemplary Woman award and a small statue. She thanked the students for their thoughtfulness, but said seriously that she did not feel she deserved the award—she would have preferred just to be present with them in the crowd, coming to learn. She gave an address setting out some of her deeply felt beliefs.

She spoke of the balance between humility and conviction:

Sometimes Mormons are considered boastful in declaring that they belong to the only true

church. But we say it not in pride, but in gratitude, considering ourselves blessed to have been born members of the Church or to have had favorable opportunity to hear the gospel preached so that we would understand and accept it. . . . We are not so arrogant as to assert that the Church program is perfect, for it continues to add programs to meet the changing times, nor would we say that its members are perfect. We have a long way to go before we have become all that the Lord wants us to be. But we do say to all who will listen, "Here is more truth than can be found anywhere else in this world, because God has established his church to teach his children as much as is within their present capacity to learn. Come, share it with us!"

Concerning woman's responsibility in the home she remarked:

So far as we know, the Church organization may not be found in heaven, but families will be. We are in a period when the great propaganda machines are telling us that for a woman to choose a career in home and family is somehow demeaning and that self-respect demands she pursue a profession of law or medicine or business. But rather than directing both marriage partners away from the home, we need to encourage both to make the strengthening of the family their primary concern. There is challenge, accomplishment, and satisfaction enough for anyone in this greatest educational endeavor—the home.

Then she told the women her philosophy on education:

The pursuit of knowledge is part of the gospel plan for men and women. My feeling is that each of us has the potential for special accomplishment in some field. The opportunities for women to excel are greater than ever before. We should all be resourceful and ambitious, expanding our interests. Forget self-pity, and look for mountains to climb. Everyone has problems. The challenge is to cope with those problems and get our full measure of joy from life. The Lord expects men and women to grow in spirituality—that is, to worship him, to gain understanding of the kind of being he is and wants us to become, to develop deep, abiding faith, and to live by divine principles of conduct.

On other occasions she dwelt on other themes. A favorite was love of God and love of neighbor as oneself. She taught that everyone should love himself—having self-respect because of a clean life, development of talents, hard work, kind deeds. Love of others would then follow, and service to others is service to God. She tried to follow her own advice and largely succeeded, but she knew it was not easy. She related once, with exasperation, her own struggles.

You know, in all my life I really disliked only one person. It was a woman I could hardly stand to speak to. She was so sickly sweet, yet so self-centered. She had nothing to talk about except her husband and her children's great accomplishments. She had no life of her own and had such vanity in the reflected glory. I find I cannot recall her without distaste. May the Lord forgive me.

For years Camilla suffered painful arthritis and rheumatism in her hands and knees. Uncomplaining, she used mild painkillers only when the discomfort became too great. A fall on the ice injured her right shoulder, so that even with cortisone shots her shoulder thereafter rarely stopped hurting. Sometimes she could not raise her arm to comb her hair, but she bore pain stoically, not wanting Spencer or others to have to worry about her.

Several times she had minor operations for removal of superficial cancers, but remembering the concern her appendectomy had caused her family, she did not tell even her children until afterward.

With their various ailments, it seemed to her as though both she and Spencer were wearing out. She had one overshadowing fear—not death, but disability. She insisted that she would not live with her children, but should be placed in a nursing home when the time came that she could not care for herself. If she had to be dependent, it would be better with strangers. She also feared the day when Spencer might feel he was no longer useful. She knew that would cast a dark cloud over both their lives. But he seemed to have great resilience.

Life was not all responsibility and problems. Spencer and Camilla had good times. Friends took them fishing in a private stocked pond. Camilla was unwilling to bait her own hook, so Hack Miller did that and cast for her, but when a trout took the bait and she pulled the good-sized fish in, she squealed in excitement. It was "great fun." And when she and Spencer visited the Church ranch in Florida several times, they both, in their mid-eighties, went horseback riding and fishing. Camilla caught several fish, "the largest bass of anyone." They watched an extemporaneous rodeo and rode through the Florida waterways on an air boat. There was something irrepressible in their spirits. For the 24th of July parade in Salt Lake City Spencer wore a Stetson and she a pioneer dress. And when an ice show came to town and they received some complimentary tickets, they rounded up a group of grandchildren to take with them.

Top, riding in BYU Centennial parade, October 1975.
Bottom, Camilla lands six-pound trout, held by Guy
Simmons, in stocked pond at Laketown, Utah, June 1977.

She liked the animated bears at Disney World and the water show at Cypress Gardens, Florida; the art show at American Fork, Utah; Shakespeare at BYU; a professional baseball game in Kansas City. She took a lesson in Japanese flower arranging and walked barefoot along the beach. She and Spencer occasionally played Mah Jongg or Rook with friends or family. When the family gathered they sang and reminisced.

In August 1977 they went to Switzerland to install a new temple presidency and to Poland to meet with government officials. Because they had several days between these appointments, Spencer asked for meetings to be arranged in other places in Europe. They held meetings in Vienna, Milan, Venice, Rome, Sicily, at St. Albans, at the temple, and in London, England. Along the way they saw the great cathedral and daVinci's *Last Supper* in Milan; rode a boat through the Grand Canal of Venice to San Marco Square; drove past the Coliseum and the Forum in Rome; suffered a multitude of mosquito bites in Sicily; and visited in London with their son Andrew, who was returning from a business trip to South Africa. From England they flew to Poland to confer with the Minister of Religion, seeking official recognition for the Church in that country. The minister, a Communist, offered them every hospitality and carefully refrained from smoking or drinking in their presence. He entertained them and arranged a trip to several cities to see places of historic importance, a museum, a monastery, public buildings, and the Orthodox Church in Warsaw for a concert.

After the concert the archbishop invited us to his home next door. I thought it was just another

At dedication of Poland to preaching of gospel, Warsaw, 1977

building to look at, and when I saw the long flight of stairs to climb I felt I could not manage with my painful knees. I asked to be excused and said I would just wait downstairs.

The priest who was with us rushed upstairs and in a moment returned with a chair for me, and three other priests to help him carry me. I was alarmed and refused vigorously; I was not going to let them carry *me* around. You've never seen me move so fast as I did climbing those stairs, sore knees or not. When I got upstairs I found they had a table set with refreshments and I was doubly embarrassed at the fuss I had stirred up.

Early the next morning a small group of Saints gathered in a nearby park and Spencer dedicated the land of Poland for the preaching of the gospel.

They traveled from Warsaw by way of Berlin to Dresden, arriving late for the meeting.

> We found a great crowd gathered at the lovely chapel. Every inch of space was taken. Because they live in East Germany, the members' contact with the Church is severely limited. They even have little Church literature. This was the first time a president of the Church had been there since President Grant. They had a fine choir and the congregation sang with great gusto. There were many young people. It was a thrilling sight to see these faithful Saints. I was glad I had the opportunity to speak to them. I could hardly keep back the tears.
>
> After the meeting we headed for West Berlin. We passed through the central part of Dresden, which is still a mass of black bombed-out buildings, never restored since the war thirty-two years ago. War is a dreadful crime against humanity; everyone loses.

It was a busy day with the dedicatory service in Warsaw at 7:00 A.M., a meeting in Dresden at 2:00 P.M., and another in Berlin at 8:00 P.M. The next morning Spencer and Camilla met with the missionaries before their flight home.

At general conference in April 1978 Spencer and Camilla again had to move to an apartment in the Hotel Utah that the Church maintained for the president. This time concern for their security arose from the ongoing trial of followers of Ervil LeBaron for the murder of Dr. Rulon Allred, leader of a polygamous group. Camilla wrote, "The apartment is beautiful, but I still feel that I am in prison."

One of the trials of Camilla's life was for people to assume she must have advance knowledge of any new development in the Church. But because of Spencer's careful maintenance of confidentiality, she knew most things only by public announcement. And, she noted, since Spencer could not always remember which matters were public and which still confidential, "He never tells me anything."

In spring 1978 she knew something weighed heavily on Spencer's mind. He was distracted, working at some problem. He fasted a great deal and spent long hours in the temple over a period of weeks. She could only speculate; she thought that perhaps one of the Church leaders was in some great difficulty. She worried over Spencer and prayed for him. She noted that in their prayers together he asked for revelation of the Lord's will more directly than she had ever heard before.

One day as she was working in the garden the telephone rang and she answered. Olive Beth asked, excitedly, "Have you heard the news?"

"What news?"

"About the revelation that all worthy men can receive the priesthood!"

Camilla turned from the telephone to her bedroom and knelt to pray, with tears of gratitude for the revelation, for the extension of blessings to more people, and for the relief that should come to her husband now that he had his answer. On her calendar she marked the day of announcement, June 8, 1978, "Red Letter Day!"

Later in 1978 they took a strenuous trip to South

Africa and South America. They went first to the
Washington, D.C., temple and then to London. They
flew on the supersonic Concorde, a marvel that
crossed the Atlantic in three and a half hours. The
plane lacked the comfort of other jets, but made up for
that in speed. A day later they flew to South Africa,
leaving England at 6:00 P.M. and arriving in Johannes-
burg at 10:00 A.M. There they began almost immediately three days of meetings. Among the more
than three thousand persons present, one group came
from Rhodesia in a caravan, armed with guns because
of the war conditions in their country. The conference
met in a huge tent, which was swelteringly hot.

The Church leaders flew to Cape Town and then
Buenos Aires, nine hours' flying time away. A few
hours later they flew on to Montevideo, where after
two days in travel they were able to bathe and clean up.

Spencer's legs pained him and he did not feel well.

I was very worried and prayed constantly that
the Lord would make him equal to the day. He
had a press conference first, then a visit with the
president of Uruguay, so he was a little late for the
first conference meeting. He spoke well at the
morning meeting. Then he conducted the afternoon meeting and spoke well as the last speaker. I
was so very grateful and much relieved. He spoke
again at the priesthood meeting. At the close they
almost had a riot with men competing to get to
him for a greeting. The mothers and daughters
meeting was held at the same time. I gave a
twenty-five-minute talk, reading it in Spanish.
The women seemed pleased and with their chil-

> dren greeted me with a kiss on the cheek. One
> little girl got to me three times through the crowd.

The next area conference convened in Buenos
Aires; then they flew to Sao Paulo for the dedication of
the new temple, the first to be completed of the new
temples Spencer had announced. Camilla was moved
by the beauty of the temple, the fine hand-carved
furniture that graced it, and the thousands of great
personal sacrifices its construction required. Ten separate dedicatory services allowed all who wished and
had recommends to participate. On the following
weekend an area conference in Sao Paulo ended the
two-and-a-half-week trip.

At the close of the conference the congregation
sang "God Be with You Till We Meet Again." Then
they stood and waved white handkerchiefs in an emotional farewell.

With plane changes, it took Spencer and Camilla
and others of their party nearly twenty-four hours to
return home, tired but grateful for the successful conferences and temple dedication.

> We ate little of the dinner on the plane. I put
> the steaks in a bag to take home. After we changed
> planes we had a meal on the next plane. I salvaged
> the sliced sandwich meat and we had meat at
> home for most of the week.

She did the same thing at a hotel banquet where
she and Spencer were guests of honor. At first she felt
some reluctance to ask the waiter for a bag to wrap the
meat in, but on second thought she did ask. The left-

over steak furnished several meals, eventually as stew. Her family always said that her meals of leftovers tasted as good as new.

Windfall fruit always had to be put up, lest it waste. Olive Beth finally resorted to throwing the worst of the fruit over the back fence to save her mother from feeling it had to be used somehow. Camilla made juice from apricots, jam from the pulp, then added the sweet pits to the jam. One day she worked from 5:00 A.M. to 10:00 P.M. bottling juice from windfall apples, leaving her completely exhausted.

Camilla bought her clothes on sale—with one exception. For a formal reception she bought a long pink dress with sequined collar at full price, and felt wickedly extravagant. She wore it ten years and later shortened it for an afternoon dress. Even when she came to the point where she did not need to economize so much, she found great satisfaction in shopping the clothing sales. In grocery shopping she would go from store to store, purchasing the sale items, carefully mapping her route so as not to spend more on gasoline than she saved on the sales.

One time she found that she had received ten cents too much change from the market. She got in her car and drove back to return the money. Despite her unquestioned honesty, however, one situation offered special challenge. Whenever she received a letter on which the stamp had not been cancelled, it took conscious struggle to throw away "the perfectly good stamp." She had to think through carefully that the stamp merely established that the postage had been paid.

For many years a nonmember family lived next door. The relationship was friendly but not close.

When the husband fell ill, Camilla and Spencer provided a ready resource for help. And after the woman,
Pauline, was widowed, Camilla offered a sympathetic
ear. Feeling that women, no less than men, have a
responsibility to share the gospel, she talked to Pauline
about the Church and offered to teach her or arrange
for teaching, but found no interest. Camilla regretted
that Pauline missed the comfort she might have had
after her husband's death through an understanding
of the gospel.

One day, as she was taking some cake next door,
Camilla received no answer to her knock. Sensing
something amiss, she tried telephoning and then
called on another neighbor who had a key to the
house. Pauline lay in the hallway, having died of a
heart attack.

For twenty-five years, from the time of their
mother's death, Camilla's deaf sister, Mary, lived in
her home. Much as Camilla loved her, she found it
hard to have another person in the house, especially
one sometimes difficult to deal with, but Camilla willingly accepted care of Mary as her responsibility.
When Mary had a cancer operation, Camilla, who was
eighty-four, felt taxed beyond her limit and her sisters
helped by taking Mary for two weeks each while she
recovered. Neither Mary nor Camilla could negotiate
the stairs to her bedroom easily. Mary recovered well
and returned to live with Camilla, but a few months
later, in 1979, she died quietly in her sleep of a heart
attack while staying overnight with her sister Caroline.

I nearly had hysterics when Caroline called
me. Rationally I am grateful Mary passed away so
peacefully, but emotionally I felt that after all

these years I had abandoned her at the last, that I
should have been with her when she died, that my
home was her home. She had been my special
charge ever since we were children, and I felt very
close to her.

We made arrangements for her funeral in the
ward for the deaf, where she had so many friends.
A large crowd of relatives and friends, including
the First Presidency and several other General
Authorities, gathered to pay Mary honor. Some of
the participants used sign language and others
spoke aloud; each was translated for the other
group. I was well satisfied with the service. We laid
her to rest near Grandmother Romney; Mary
would be pleased.

In the summer of 1979 Camilla and Spencer visited
the Church ranch in Florida again. When they went
horseback riding this time she needed a ladder to
mount. As they rode through the pastures and groves
on the ranch, they saw deer and wild hogs. She enjoyed
being out-of-doors, but she always wore a broad hat to
protect her fair skin.

Camilla returned to find that her garden had suffered and the hot wind had cost her half her petunias.
Mary was no longer there to keep the yard watered
when they were away. Camilla bottled eleven quarts of
cherries that her sister Rose brought her and also
made raspberry jam.

In July they went to California for a convention of
the Church-owned Beneficial Life Company. Shortly
before Spencer was to speak he suddenly felt dizzy.
Camilla motioned to Dr. Taylor, who checked Spencer
briefly and then, when he insisted on speaking, helped

Church News Photo

*At the Church ranch in
Florida, 1980*

Church News Photo

him to the lectern. When he examined Spencer more
carefully later, the doctor thought it not a stroke but

perhaps a precursor to a stroke. She wrote, "It was a tense time. I was very worried. I have great anxiety about the possibility of this dread calamity. I slept little through the night."

As soon as they returned to Salt Lake City they went directly to the hospital for examination. Spencer had slight impairment on his left side, but was showing quick improvement. Dr. Nelson concluded that likely the problem was shedding of dacron fibers from the artificial heart valve that had been installed seven years before. These fibers clogged tiny blood vessels, and if it happened in the hand it might produce numbness, or if in the brain, dizziness. After a few days' monitoring in the hospital, Spencer was able to return home, but he suffered a continuing oppressive weariness. Then another similar episode occurred; this time, though the recurrence was unsettling since it suggested a whole series of such attacks, he did not go to the hospital and the effects passed away in a few days.

Camilla took care of Spencer devotedly, but she had trouble dealing with his feeling depressed about his condition. In Toronto when he experienced difficulty, he turned his talk over to his secretary, Arthur Haycock, to read. The problem was partly with his eyes; glaucoma and cataracts interfered with his reading, and he had to have his talks typed in large print. Even that was sometimes not enough. At other times it seemed that his eyesight improved and he could manage even ordinary print.

At BYU to give a devotional address to 25,000 in the Marriot Center, Spencer again had to ask President Dallin Oaks to finish reading his talk. The next day he had difficulty walking. Camilla wrote, "Spencer has not been even as well as usual. I am worried." His brother-in-law George Nelson died in Brigham City and he and Camilla drove there the next day to visit his sister Alice, the only other surviving member of his family. Spencer was so weak that he required help to dress himself, and in Brigham City he had to be helped in walking, though he acted cheerful in company.

Before they returned to Salt Lake City Arthur Haycock telephoned the doctor and arranged for Spencer to be taken directly for examination. Dr. Wilkinson then had him driven to the hospital, and testing began. Within a few hours Dr. Bruce Sorensen, a neurologist, concluded that Spencer had a subdural hematoma, a collection of blood and fluid between the skull and the brain, pressing on the brain and disrupting his motor functions. The prospect without operation was death.

The operation took place at once. At one in the morning Dr. Sorensen drilled a pencil-size hole in the skull and opened the brain covering. The pressure was so great that fluid spurted out two feet. Camilla sat tensely awaiting word. The doctors gave a hopeful report. If all went well, Spencer should recover completely. He might even be able to appear at general conference, a month away, though he could not expect to participate much. Such a hematoma usually occurs from some sort of blow to the head that starts hemorrhaging inside the skull, but neither of them could recall any sharp blows. Sometimes the bleeding and increase in fluid pressure is very slow, only discovered when fluids have built up substantially. The surgeon removed three-fourths of a cup of fluid.

Camilla spent what time she was allowed beside Spencer's bed in the intensive care unit, a noisy, distressing place where several patients struggled for life.

She had to deal with Spencer's sequence of nightmares and hallucinations and discomfort and depression, "so unlike him." Soon he was transferred to a regular hospital room, and she could go home for a few hours at a time to pick the beans and tomatoes to give to her neighbors or freeze or bottle. She also put up pears and peaches. Spencer insisted that most of the flowers he received should be distributed to other patients in the hospital.

While Spencer remained hospitalized, Camilla attended the Churchwide conference for women and read Spencer's message to them. "I felt it a real privilege," she said.

At home she baked six loaves of bread and pickled beets from her yard. "I hope it will be a long time before either of us has to come to the hospital again."

After two weeks Spencer returned home. A security man was stationed inside the house at all times to help him if needed. A few days later their grandson Tom Mack married. Spencer attended the sealing ceremony but did not feel equal to attending the wedding reception. Camilla went without him. When she went to receptions with Spencer she willingly went to the head of the line, if invited to do so, knowing that otherwise Spencer would be unable to attend at all. But since she was not with him that evening she stood in the long line, visiting with people, despite urgings from other guests and from usher-grandsons that she go ahead.

Spencer soon insisted on going to his office. Camilla always worried about his overextending himself, but she had long since learned that her protests would have little effect. At conference time he said, "I am determined to give leadership to the conference," and he not only attended, he also spoke five times. He spoke more briefly than usual and did so with difficulty, yet he would not be deterred. She worried, but she admired his determination.

They had assumed that a scheduled trip to Israel to dedicate the Orson Hyde Memorial Garden would have to be delegated to others, but as the time approached they decided to go. Just a few days after general conference they flew to London and Athens and boarded a ship that sailed through the Greek isles and to Egypt. The ship carried a BYU tour group. Camilla loved the shipboard lectures on art and history and religion. She and Spencer watched movies and visited. Some nights they rested well; other times Spencer tossed restlessly. In Egypt they drove through the delta and watched farmers working in the age-old primitive ways and women doing their washing in the canals.

The ship sailed on to Israel, and they toured again through the Holy Land, seeing sights they had seen before. They felt a special poignancy this time, however, since it seemed likely they would not come again. They thoroughly enjoyed the trip, but Camilla noted:

> We have walked up and down so many stairs and hills my knees are "worn to the bone." Spencer's legs hurt; my miserable knees get more painful every day. People have been very kind to help the "old folks" get around. I am so grateful Spencer was well enough to make this historic trip. He has stood the trip well and is definitely better than when we left.

The dedication itself capped their visit. Civic

With Dr. Ernest Wilkinson outside ice cream parlor in Greece, 1979

leaders, Church leaders, and about two thousand persons crowded the Orson Hyde Memorial Garden for the dedicatory service. Spencer's prayer recalled the occasion of Orson Hyde's dedication of the land for the gathering of Abraham's scattered children and prayed for the protection of the garden as a place of peace.

They flew from Israel to Switzerland, where Spencer met with the temple presidency. Camilla remarked of the countryside, from where her grandmother Eyring had come:

> The landscape was beautiful beyond description—green fields, lush gardens, wooded areas

ablaze with fall colors, despite a chilly fog. Many things are old, but everything seems very clean and in perfect repair. Every inch of ground is frugally used.

November 16, their sixty-second wedding anniversary, proved to be "a sad day." Numbness in Spencer's left hand and arm signified trouble, and a new brain scan confirmed that fluid had collected again inside the skull in the same area as before. Another operation, entering through the already-drilled hole, removed the fluid. He had gone into the operation in good spirits, joking, "I hope they don't start without me," which Camilla found comforting, but seeing her husband struggle even more than the first time through the distressing days of intensive care and slow recovery was almost more than she could bear. She noted: "This is the most traumatic experience of my life. I have been crying my eyes out. I hope and pray I will be privileged to take care of my darling as long as he lives."
Camilla slept on a pallet beside his bed.

He went to bed after medication. At nine in the morning I roused him and asked if he would like to hear the Tabernacle Choir. He sat up in a chair but immediately went to sleep and could not be aroused. The physiotherapist came to give him exercises but could not rouse him enough to get a response. I became increasingly concerned. He acted as if he had been drugged. I knelt by his bed with his hand in mine pleading with the Lord and weeping endlessly. Olive Beth came after the choir broadcast and I was in tears. I began to feel he was going to just sink away. At my request the nurse called Dr. Wilkinson, and when he came and investigated, he found that Spencer had been given a sedative rather than a blood pressure pill. It was a great relief to know that "this, too, would pass." By evening he began to come out of it. I could not have been more distraught if he had really gone.

Spencer seemed quite himself again by the next day, and he walked a bit through the halls. A week later he was able to return home. He seemed stronger than after the first brain surgery.

It takes more than a little will power for me to keep cheerful when Spencer is melancholy. The arthritis in my knees gets increasingly worse and my shoulder is more painful all the time. At home I am nurse, housekeeper, cook, and hostess, which I am not always equal to. Sometimes I wonder how long I can keep up. I try hard not to let Spencer know how miserable I sometimes feel.

After a week at home Spencer went to the office for the first time and Camilla attended a luncheon.

I had a holiday, the first time I had been in company for three weeks. I had my hair done. It needed it badly and it gave me a lift to look respectable again. I also met with the general Primary board. I gave my talk, which was well received. They called me up with two of the board members who were having December birthdays also. The group sang "Happy Birthday" to the three of us. I appreciated it. This was one of the

most special days I have had in years. I really felt
exhilarated after my long siege of anxiety with
Spencer's illness.

The next day she noted:

This is my eighty-fifth birthday. I spent it
cleaning house. Olive Beth brought me a supply
of frozen orange juice, which I have stopped
buying because it is more than twice as expensive
as it was before inflation.

Then a few days later Spencer had to return to the
hospital for the fourth time since July with a problem
of blood imbalance. The doctors' task was to keep it
thin enough so it would not clot and cause a stroke, yet
thick enough to avoid yet another hemorrhage. For
some reason Spencer had the hiccups for four days.
He received the blood medication by continuous in-
travenous injection, so he was tied to a bottle of saline
solution by tubes. When he walked through the hallway for exercise there was a great procession—
Spencer, a rolling stand with the apparatus connected
to him, a nurse, a security man, and Camilla, with
people standing by watching the parade. Everyone
wanted to greet them.

In five days Spencer returned home once more
and Camilla could turn her attention to preparations
for the Christmas celebration. The love people had for
them and the respect for their position resulted in a
shower of gifts of food and flowers. The most striking
was a forty-three-pound turkey that Camilla cooked
for seventeen hours in preparation for Christmas dinner. She prepared dinner for thirty family members

*Camilla, Spencer, Olive Beth, and
great-grandchildren, 1977*

who gathered in her home to celebrate not only the
birth of Christ but also their gratitude for the miracle
of survival.

It was wonderful to have our loved ones
gathered around us. They are a comfort and
blessing. I get great pleasure from watching them
move ahead with their lives, developing physical-
ly, mentally, and spiritually. Next to our relationship with the Lord, they are the most important
thing in our lives. Being with them offers a fore-
taste of heaven.

Epilogue

An interviewer for a magazine said to Camilla, "It seems to me that with all you've been through, you are entitled to feel depressed."

Camilla responded emphatically, "Of course there are moments of discouragement, but if you have the impression that trouble is the main theme in my life, you are mistaken. I have had a wonderful life. I have been blessed with righteous parents, a loving husband and family, generous neighbors, and stimulating friends. Spencer and I have received respect and honor. I have had challenging responsibilities and a sense of being useful to the Lord's work in at least a small way. Others suffer their share of trials too; their troubles are just different from mine. I learned long ago that with God's help there is no difficulty too great to overcome. That knowledge keeps me from being discouraged for long. Life is eternal, and our present experiences simply serve as preparation for what is to come. We cannot afford to sink into self-pity. We have too much to learn and do.

"I love this life. I love the hot sun on my back as I work in the garden; I love to gather my family about me; I love parties; I love to read and to explore ideas and see new places; I love to visit the Saints and sense their vibrant faith. Living in this world has proven to be a voyage of continual discovery. I am reluctant to have it end. I am having too good a time."

Index